Oh. I'm A Widow

Working Through Life After a Death

Barbara Rady Kazdan

Culicidae Press®
PO Box 5069
Madison, WI 53705-5069
culicidaepress.com
editor@culicidaepress.com

OH. I'M A WIDOW: WORKING THROUGH LIFE AFTER A DEATH
Copyright © 2025 by Barbara Rady Kazdan
All rights reserved.

No part of this book may be reproduced in any form by any electronic or mechanized means (including photocopying, recording, or information storage and retrieval) without written permission, except in the case of brief quotations embodied in critical articles and reviews. For more information, please visit culicidaepress.com

ISBN: 978-1-68315-113-5

Library of Congress Control Number: 2024952753

Our books may be purchased in bulk for promotional, educational or business use. Please contact your local bookseller or the Culicidae Press Sales Department at +1-352-215-7558 or by email at sales@culicidaepress.com

x.com/culicidaepress – facebook.com/culicidaepress
threads.net/@culicidaepress – instagram.com/culicidaepress
culicidaepress.bsky.social

Design by polytekton © 2025
Cover image generated by Midjourney AI system and modified by polytekton

Acknowledgements

This book is dedicated to my father, whose values shaped mine; my mother, whose unfailing optimism I carry; my sister, whose resilience I admire; my children, whose love and support sustain me every day of my life; and my grandchildren, who bring me joy, laughter and faith in the future.

I'm grateful to David Mezzapelle, who invited me to contribute personal essays to two anthologies, *Contagious Optimism* and *10 Habits of Truly Optimistic People*, opening my way to a challenging and fulfilling encore career.

Sometimes one person can change the course of your life. After attending a writing workshop led by Sara Taber, we walked to the parking lot together. She asked, "Would you like to join my memoir group?"

That small, supportive group of talented writers became and remains my writing home. In their company I've explored my journey from the shock of widowhood to a full new life. I'm grateful for Sara's validation of my work, her guidance in honing my craft, and her belief in the value my story offers to women experiencing widowhood.

TABLE OF CONTENTS

Acknowledgements	3
Introduction	6
Phase One	**10**
She Brought Her Knitting	12
Home, Please	25
Goodbyes	32
The Mourning Fog	38
In Sickness and In Health	47
Identity Loss	58
Remembering	63
Phase Two	**68**
Get Up, Get Dressed, Now What?	70
No New Messages	73
I've Lost That Special Feeling	79
My Geographically Challenged Family	83
The Presence of Absence	88
Phase Three	**92**
Lonely? You're Not Alone	94
Kissing a Lot of Frogs…	99
Staying Single? Suits Me!	105
Searching for Community	109

Phase Four	**116**
Coming Into My Own	116
Looking Back, Moving Forward	117
Who, Me? Change the Filter, Drain the Pipes?	119
A Creative Path to Kindred Spirits	124
Taking the Wheel, Steering My Course	129
My New Backup Team	132
I Can Do That Myself!	140
Phase Five	**148**
A Bad Case of Being Stuck	150
Retired Executive—Will Work for Smiles	154
Paddling Upstream and Down	157
Here Comes Life—I Hope You Like Surprises	165
The Tree and Me	171
Afterword	**174**

Introduction

Although each new widow must find her own way, most will encounter daunting emotional and practical challenges. Similarly, each post-retirement odyssey, while charted by the individual, navigates well-traveled passages. I lost my husband of 42 years just after I'd stepped down from a high-profile, career-culminating position.

As I emerged from the cocoon of grief, I faced two challenges: finding intellectual engagement and rebuilding my personal life. One serendipitous invitation led me to a new professional calling and a congenial, supportive peer group.

After a few years of consulting and serving on nonprofit boards, I felt like a race car used only for Sunday drives. Then, out of the blue, someone I'd encountered professionally invited me to contribute to *Contagious Optimism*, an anthology of personal essays.

"May I write about my personal life?"

"Sure."

Intrigued, I wrote about what was top of mind: my experiences as a new widow. All of my essays were accepted! Some are included in this book.

In my career, writing was a strength I'd relied on to gain support for nonprofit initiatives. As I embarked on my life as a widow, writing offered me a way to reflect on and share my journey.

Over lunch one day I told my friend Isabelle, a longtime Washingtonian, "You know that invitation to contribute to an anthology of upbeat stories? They accepted all the essays I submitted!"

"That's great! One of the best writing centers is nearby, in Bethesda. You should check out their workshops."

I did. After the summer session ended, the instructor and I walked out together.

"Would you like to join a memoir group that meets in my home?"

Bingo! That invitation yielded a new, all-in pursuit, and supportive fellow writers, a group sharing the most personal, close-to-the-bone stories of our lives and—over time—coming to care about each other.

Encouraged, I began studying the craft in the memoir group. Is writing a full-time gig now? Not quite. But happily, my work has been published in journals and online publications. Does it pay? Not often, and not much. But writing helps me answer the dreaded question, "What do you do?" That matters to me. For decades I'd defined myself largely by my work. More than that, I needed to have a purpose and hear an occasional "good job." Like my life as an at-home mom, retirement offers no milestones to reach, no measures of progress. When my essays are published, I get that missing ingredient from readers, like these comments about a piece describing my progress from grieving widow to the engaged, vibrant life I enjoy today:

- I can relate! Divorced after twenty-eight years, I, too, celebrated everything from buying a car on my own to changing a furnace filter. I joined a choir and found a new tribe. Thanks for reminding me how far I've come.
- For thirty-five years I've leaned on my husband for house, car and financial matters—thought I could never manage on my own. Now I know I can.

Those messages are gratifying. And validating.

This book recounts my jagged journey from the shock of widowhood and the pesky persistence of loneliness to the discovery of new people, new pursuits, and a full life. Looking back at the years since my husband Dan died, I've observed distinct phases of experience and growth, all moving toward an engaged and fulfilling life. I describe them in the following pages.

I hope my story will be helpful and hopeful to widows and offer insights to those supporting them.

Phase One

Stunned, Suddenly Single

On the day my husband died I was too numb to think clearly. One calm, caring friend helped me identify and attend to the formalities. Despite a numbness that had settled over me, there were decisions to make and tasks that couldn't wait. Soon flights arrived, bringing our three children to our suburban D.C. home to comfort me and each other.

After a memorial service the next morning, our family broke bread together before our eldest daughter Sandra and her husband had to get back to their children. Jenna, our second-born daughter, stayed a week (her husband had stayed home with their son). Jake, our youngest, stayed another week. After he left, for the first time in over forty years, I was on my own.

She Brought Her Knitting

Early that December morning, Dan called, "Bye, I'm going to the store."

"Okay," I called from my desk in the upstairs office, typing away to capture a morning brainstorm.

Several minutes later I noticed that our dog Toto was dashing back and forth between me and the front door. Curious, I went to the door and peeked out. What I saw shocked me into action: The car was running and Dan was in the driver's seat, but he'd never left the driveway. I rushed out into the frigid air, dialing 911 as I approached the car.

His blank stare shocked me. I felt numb.

In minutes the emergency team arrived and went to work. They laid my husband on the driveway, baring his chest to start CPR. Flat on his back on the cold pavement my big-bellied husband looked like a defenseless beached whale. Caught up in their frenzied efforts, suddenly I realized: *Oh my God, he's gone!*

Unable to revive Dan, the medics transferred him to the ambulance. The driver's words confirmed my worst fear: "Why don't you ride with me?"

I knew what that meant. I wouldn't be in any shape to drive myself home.

At the hospital I was ushered into a small, private room with institutional-green cinder block walls, an upholstered bench and a molded plastic pull-up chair. I sat on the bench, stunned, dazed, stomach clenched. A slim, grey-haired black woman introduced herself gently as Reverend somebody, the hospital chaplain. She pulled up the chair to face me. After a longer-than-expected wait, an ER doctor appeared, telling me what I expected but wasn't prepared to hear—is anyone, ever?

"We did everything we could, but we were unable to revive him. I'm so sorry, but your husband died."

I sat there.

Motionless.

Mute.

The chaplain sat with me as I listened to the doctor. She explained that I could see Dan in a few minutes. I knew that Dan was at risk of a life-threatening event; he'd been hospitalized more than once, emerging each time less vital, more fragile, but more determined to live—mostly to enjoy the grandchildren he loved. Just ten months before, after a sirens-blaring trip to the hospital and a gut-wrenching night I spent in the ER while a medical team struggled to stabilize him, I'd sat at his bedside during the ten-day hospitalization that followed, watching his vital signs swing from scary to steady and back again. Before he came home, weakened, Dan spent two weeks in rehab. Since then he'd been taking his meds and seeing his doctors regularly—always with good reports. He was optimistic. But our children and I worried. The news I was about to share wouldn't come as a complete surprise.

Then a panel next to the blank wall opened, and a neck-high, sheet-covered pallet bearing my husband's body rolled out into the room. Was he at peace? No! His reddened, puffed-up face looked like he'd just gone ten rounds in a boxing ring. A big drop of blood graced his lips. *They couldn't take one more second to wipe the blood away?* He was anything but at peace.

Regretting that I'd called 911 and put him through pointless, exhaustive last-ditch measures, I kissed his bruised, still-warm lips.

Said goodbye.

Prayed that his spirit was light years away from his physical remains.

Wished that this moment could be private, anywhere but in this cold, sterile setting.

I had no sense of time, but after a while the pallet bearing his body slid back into the opening in the wall. Then he was gone. Even though I'd known this day was coming, my whole being rocked with shock.

"I'm so sorry," the chaplain said, as my tears flowed and sobs escaped my chest.

Pulling myself together, I called each of our children.

"Honey, I'm at the hospital," I said to Sandra, our firstborn, her father's favorite. "Daddy had a heart attack this morning. He's gone. He didn't suffer."

Choking out the words, I delivered this impossibly difficult, still unbelievable message twice more, following our children's birth order. Aware that losing their father would affect each one in a deeply personal way, I heard loss, not shock, in their voices. They knew that their dad, overweight and sedentary, had been living at high risk for years, but they were not prepared to let him go. Each had their own memories of Dan. Sandra, closest to him and like him a planner, list maker, and realist; Jenna, thoughtful, supportive, and resourceful; and self-directed, life-embracing Jake, who'd arrived later in our lives to a disengaged but caring dad. After hanging up from those calls, I knew the children would be making their ways to our—I mean my—home in Maryland. We needed to be together.

⁂

After the last call, the chaplain asked. "May I call someone to take you home?"

It had been four years since we'd moved from Houston, our home for twenty-eight years, to our suburban DC house. Until recently I'd commuted daily to a demanding job and traveled often for work. Dan would drive me to the METRO in the morning and pick me up at night. We'd catch up over dinner before settling in for an evening of TV:

"Talk to the kids today?"

"Yes, Anna went down the slide by herself today."

"Big girl!"

"Did you make the deadline for that proposal?"

"Barely."

Caught up in the high-pressure work-is-all D.C. scene, my inbox often overflowed, spilling into my personal time. On weekends we'd head over to Jenna's to enjoy the new baby. We hadn't begun to make social connections.

Who could come to the hospital to pick me up that morning? The only friends I had were former colleagues who would be at work, an hour away. My neighbors were an elderly woman and a young mother with babies.

Who could the chaplain call? Seeing her distress, I strained to come up with a name.

"I can't think of anyone."

Her expression signaled: Wrong answer!

"Are you sure? I'd hate to put you in a taxi by yourself."

"I'm sure."

Reluctantly, this kind, gentle woman took my hand, led me to the exit, and put me in a cab for a solo journey home. I'd never felt more alone.

On the way, it occurred to me, *Maybe Kay could come.* My longtime yoga teacher, she lived nearby. Her schedule changed from day to day.

I called.

"I'll be there in 10 minutes."

When she arrived, after a much-needed hug, I saw that she'd brought her knitting. Oh. My shoulders dropped; my breathing slowed. She intended to stay. Nothing could have been more reassuring.

Kay, warm brown eyes framed by greying shoulder-length curls, took in the situation. "What do we have to do?" she asked, in the gentle voice I'd listened to during years of yoga classes.

I heard that 'we' with enormous relief. There was so much to do—find a funeral home, plan a memorial service, figure out who'd meet each of the children's planes…Together, we tackled a myriad of time-sensitive tasks.

Kay led me through that frenzied day, making and fielding calls, figuring out what we needed to do, keeping notes. We had to work fast. It was Thursday. Because I'm Jewish, I told Kay that the service had to be before sundown Friday. Oh, how I needed—but had not yet found—a rabbi who knew and cared about me. A rush of sadness and anxiety swept over me. Dan and I hadn't affiliated with a congregation. Who would officiate at the memorial service?

"We don't have a congregation," I said. "We've been going to services led by a rabbi-without-a-pulpit."

"Call him."

"I'm sorry, I'm not available," he said, but suggested a few colleagues.

Before I could start those calls, the phone rang; a familiar, deep, southern-accented voice said: "Barbara, I'm still your rabbi. What happened?"

Beyond time and geography, it was our rabbi calling from Houston, the rabbi who'd consecrated each of our children as they'd started Sunday School kindergarten; presided over the Bat and Bar Mitzvahs and confirmations of each of our three children; come to our home for the bris of our newborn son, officiated at our daughter's weddings, and comforted us when we grieved the passing of our parents. That voice on the other end of the phone line brought a wave of relief but surfaced the longing that vied with grief for emotional top billing throughout that day. I hadn't realized till I heard his voice how much I craved my connection to this friend and spiritual anchor, someone who knew and cared about me. And Dan. And our children. A man whose children had grown up with ours. Someone who understood. And a link to the prime of our lives when Dan and I were celebrating our own and our children's life passages. I clung to his words like a child clinging to a parent's hand.

After that time-shifting, heart-soothing call, I continued my calls to local rabbis.

"We have a rabbi," I told Kay, as I hung up the phone. "He sounds nice. He'll conduct the service tomorrow morning."

Then we tackled the next question: What funeral home to use? A former colleague with ties to the Jewish community answered that question.

That day Kay and I learned the ins and outs of all these arrangements and more. Each contact, with the funeral home, the rabbi, and others, brought up more questions for which I had no ready answers. Over and over again, Kay helped me make difficult choices.

It was urgent to decide who needed to be called and by whom. Kay made lists, compiled a phone roster, assigned tasks to my family and hers, kept track of time, knew what we'd done and what remained to do. I took the calls I wanted or needed to; Kay fielded the rest.

Another task: tracking travel logistics. As we noted and kept track of the children's arrival times, I thought about each one's relationship with Dan, as children and adults. What were they feeling, thinking, remembering? I pictured them: Jake—his Hollywood-handsome face framed with endearing dark curls, easygoing with a lightning-fast wit. Buoyant Jake, gobbling up life with gusto, carving out a screenwriting career in L.A. Jake, who'd arrived a decade after his siblings, just as Dan had begun retreating from life. How would he mourn the dad whose fulsome engagement he'd never enjoyed? Jenna, slender with warm hazel eyes and medium brown curls, self-directed even as a teen, content and competent as a wife, mom, and manager of sweeping social research projects. Jenna, so like me—intuitive, keeping her options open—so different from her dad and siblings. Would she be reflecting on her troubled but long-resolved relationship with Dan? Sandra, first to grab and claim Dan's heart, most in tune with and, in recent years, protective of him. Sandra—tender-hearted, a stunner with prematurely grey hair and blue-eyed, lightly freckled face—often more knowledgeable than so-called experts, tapping that expertise to advocate for her children and the environment.

Dan and I had raised three open-hearted, life-embracing, caring children.

All of us had known that Dan's health was fragile. That didn't lessen our profound loss.

Kay's voice broke my reverie:

"Who'll meet Jenna's plane?"

"She said she'll rent a car."

"Who's getting Jake? He's coming in at midnight."

Kay enlisted her son for that assignment.

Sandra called: "Mom, I can't get there till the morning. My plane gets in at 10 a.m. Our neighbor will take the kids after school and keep them overnight. Ron will fly in after work tomorrow. He'll rent a car."

Relaying this to Kay, I said, "I'll ask Jake to meet Sandra's plane. She'll be a wreck; he'll be the most comforting to her."

As we sat in the living room on the plush, well-used sectional sofa next to Dan's brown tweed easy chair, surrounded by framed family photos on the parquet-topped walnut cocktail table, antique mahogany desk and shelf-like sill of a large picture window, we had three phones going, my land line and each of our cell phones. All three rang all day long.

At 4 p.m. Kay realized I hadn't eaten all day. She called a time out. That's when it hit me—I was exhausted.

"Here," she said, sitting me down at the breakfast table. "Have this."

The cup of yogurt and blueberries she offered was as soothing as chicken soup.

⁓⁓

Dan died at Holy Cross Hospital in Silver Spring, Maryland in the early morning of that cold, grey December day. Jenna, who'd moved to Phoenix, 2,500 miles away, was getting her son ready for kindergarten when she got my call. Swinging into action, she caught an early plane and miraculously rushed into my arms late that afternoon. Tears co-mingled on our cheeks. Then she sat, scanned our lists, added her phone to ours, and dove in.

Sandra called again, "Mom, what's the phone number of the event planner you worked with—Ron wants to ask her to help him organize the food for tomorrow."

Ron came on the line, "Mom, how are you holding up? I'm so sorry. He loved deli; we'll do that."

Kay reminded us, "The funeral home's closing soon."

Jenna went with me to make the arrangements. Remembering past encounters with these establishments, I steeled myself, ready to fend off salesy tactics. Dan had wanted to be cremated to avoid costly, cumbersome, creepy funeral arrangements and a burial plot in a city that wasn't home to him or to our children.

"No, we don't want a funeral. Yes, we'll need death certificates."

They gave me a tall memorial candle designed to burn throughout the week of shiva, and a bunch of brochures. About to make a hasty exit, in a cruel 'not-so-fast' moment, we heard, "You'll have to come back later to identify the body. We haven't received your husband's remains."

He chose cremation. I said goodbye in the hospital. They're saying I need to view his body again?

Jenna volunteered, "I'll go. It'll give me a chance to say goodbye." A godsend.

Back at home we continued working through the checklist. One call at the end of that long day stands out as the most stressful.

Kay said, "You have to take this one."

I picked up the phone and heard, "This is Karen, from Donate Life Maryland. Your husband is an organ donor. I need to get some information."

"Could you call back later," I whispered into the receiver, "This is a difficult time."

I had long since exhausted my reserve energy.

"No, she insisted. This is time sensitive. We have to do it now."

I wanted to respect Dan's wishes, so I forced myself to answer what seemed like an endless questionnaire about every aspect of my husband's medical history and lifestyle. He was sixty-eight. There was a lot to tell. How I wanted to escape this long, distressing call.

"Go ahead," I mumbled.

Do you approve the donation of his retinas?"

"Yes."

Really? Why is this happening? His license showed he's a donor."

"His skin?"

They're asking about his skin? I can't do this!

Answering robotically, the conversation hurtled me back to that dreary cinder block room in the hospital: *This is happening: Dan's dead!*

Days later someone from this agency called to tell me that they'd only been able to use his corneas. Information I didn't want to hear or need to know.

Throughout that day Kay had comforted me, tended to me, and steadied me. Through phone conversations she 'met' my family and friends and was the point person for the help that poured in from them.

Since our move to the D.C. area, I hadn't thought much about building a social network. I'd been completely absorbed in my challenging, rewarding but all-consuming work. But from the moment I'd found Dan in the car that morning I'd felt utterly, shockingly alone. Thankfully, I learned that day that I was far from alone. Kay, this one wonderful friend at my side, called and pulled together my widely dispersed family and friends. Asking for help had opened the way for an extraordinary woman to share that dreadful day with me.

Someone other than Kay might have made a perfunctory appearance, attended to some immediate needs, and left as soon as she could to escape the sadness and spare herself the grim tasks at hand. Not Kay. I knew that she was there for me in the fullest sense and as long as needed because... she brought her knitting.

Home, Please

Home is a place you grow up wanting to leave and grow old wanting to get back to.

John Ed Pearce

As I drove away from the hospital, a longing for home swelled up inside me.

Home.

How I wanted to go there. But where was it? Somehow over a lifetime of changing circumstances, 'For Rent' or 'For Sale' signs had sprung up, first on Dan's and my childhood homes, next on the homes we'd shared as newlyweds, and then the homes we'd made for our children. We'd watched with aching hearts as some predictable and other, jolting life events had made our children and ourselves into a benign, present-day version of what our grandparents, fleeing tyranny, had been: displaced persons.

Where was home? Not Chicago, where we'd begun married life, to be in close proximity to my newly widowed mother and a half-day drive to Dan's parents in suburban Detroit. No. Our parents had retired and moved to the Sunbelt, leaving us freezing through impossibly long, harsh winters; so, we no longer had family nearby. We'd tried to engage with couples our age but most of those we met had grown up in Chicago, married, and settled down there. Family and old friends kept their social calendars full. There was little to hold us in Chicago, so, as our children approached school age we decided to move to Houston. We'd visited our sisters in Dallas, enjoyed the mild year-round climate, and wanted the girls to grow up near their cousins, aunts, and uncles. Dan had asked for a transfer to Dallas, but the company needed him in Houston, where the economy was booming, and Dan's company was growing so fast that they offered to buy our home in Chicago and pay for our move.

"Let's do it," we'd agreed. "We'll be close enough to Dallas for the children to develop relationships with their aunts, uncles, and cousins, and to celebrate holidays with family."

Houston—an unlikely place for us to land, where our Midwestern accents made us sound like foreigners. But that's where we planted our family flag. And it was good. The children thrived in the sunny-every-day climate, and we connected with young couples like us who'd left colder, older, recession-hit cities for Houston's booming economy. Then, two decades later, with empty bedrooms where we'd once sung lullabies, we hugged goodbye our almost-family Houston friends and moved again, this time to suburban D.C.

Why the move? Although our children called Houston home, Dan and I never did. Like many empty nesters, the most mobile age group in our mobile society, some of our close friends had retired and moved away. Our ties to Houston were fraying.

What lured us to D.C.? Proximity to our daughter Jenna, newly wed to Jonathan, and the chance for me to lead the new U.S. program of an international nonprofit. Unlike our transfer to Houston, this time it was my career, not Dan's, that prompted our move.

My work was exciting but demanding, spilling over from the office to home. Frequent business travel further diminished my time with Dan, but he loved hearing about my experiences, and, as he always had, served as a sounding board for my work-related issues.

One bonus of the move: my new salary. And, later that year, being present at the birth of our first grandson, Gene. A thrill for us, and a much-needed lift for Dan who loved playing with his new grandbaby at Jenna's. Often on weekends Jenna and I would take Gene to a playground, then meet the guys for an early dinner at a family-friendly restaurant. What a welcome change it was for us, for our families, to celebrate birthdays and holidays together! We made memories, like watching Gene enjoy his birthday party at a fire station with seven little ones wearing pint-sized firefighters' hats.

Then, five years after we'd moved to the area, Jenna announced that she and her family were moving to Phoenix.

Beyond shocked, Dan and I struggled to process what felt like a cruel turn of events. Her siblings protested: "They can't do that!" But our son-in-law Jonathan's health required a dry climate. We couldn't argue with that. Six months later, off they went.

So, on the day Dan died, I had no family nearby and only a passing acquaintance with our neighbors. Without my husband's presence, the house I returned to as a new widow that day, was simply that—a house. Home—that comforting space where those dearest to me and unconditional love resided, no longer had a physical location.

What to do with the longing to go home? Archie Bunker would have said, in his classic catchphrase, "Stifle it." Easier to say than do. I pushed that strong longing out of my mind, but it took up permanent residence in my psyche.

As that long, life-changing day and the next unfolded, the suburban D.C. house that Dan and I had shared filled with beloved faces. One, then another of our children, and then the third took wing from three states in three time zones and swooped into my arms to comfort me and to find comfort. The older two would return to the homes they'd made in Arizona and North Carolina. Jake, the youngest, a single twenty-something, had moved from one West Coast address to another as opportunities beckoned. Jake was a preteen when his sisters left for college, so during and after his school years, he and I had become travel buddies and developed a special closeness as we explored places far from his Houston birthplace.

On that day when everything in me yearned for home, the home I pictured was with my mother, father, and sister, steps away from grandpa and grandma's place, nestled in a neighborhood where people stayed from cradle to grave, where we walked to the grocer, the butcher, and the baker, all of whom greeted us by name. When out and about, we bumped into neighbors who, like us, saw each other and their extended family often, at each other's homes, at the park, or at their places of worship. Many lived on the same block or in the same apartment building as members of their extended family. *That* was home.

In the film *Lion*, a five-year-old boy in rural India falls asleep on an empty train and wakes up several days later in Calcutta. Adopted by an Australian family, the boy, with only vague memories of the place where he was born, can't let go of the need to find that village and his birth mother. At mid-life, flashbacks bring long-buried memories that eventually lead him home. In late life, I flash back, too—in dreams and in a deep longing for that two-bedroom, one-bath sanctuary on Chicago's north side where love abided.

Years ago, as each of my children prepared to leave the nest, I'd tell them, tongue in cheek, "No worry. Wherever you live, I'll live next door." A wisecrack with an undercurrent of wishful thinking.

Although my children keep in close touch, by choice, chance, and circumstance, they live far apart from each other. Sandra (on the east coast) and her brother Jake (on the opposite coast) see each other often. I'm hoping that Sandra will move to LA someday. Then maybe I'll move there to be with two of my three chickadees and closer to the third in Phoenix. Though it won't be my home, maybe *I'll* bring *them* the sense of home they had while growing up, and I'll recapture the joy of sharing my life with them.

Recently, Jake and I were talking about his future plans.

"Remember when we talked about sharing a duplex someday?" I asked.

"Sure," he said. "Maybe we will."

Oh. He hasn't given up on living near family again. Why should I?

I know what you're thinking: a young family with a mother/mother-in-law under the same roof could be a recipe for disaster, even with a wall dividing their residences. Hey— I'm looking for a safe haven, not a slice of heaven. Even if a dash of dissonance occasionally intrudes, Jake and I, having lived away from family for so long, would like to try it. Though far from the sense of home I had as a child, at this stage of life I'd love to live with family again and give my youngest grandchildren the unconditional love my grandparents gave me. These children would have what so many families have lost, the experience of intergenerational living. Just the possibility of this gave me some comfort as I adjusted to the silence and solitude of life without Dan.

Goodbyes

On the day Dan died, Jake left Los Angeles and arrived at the house before bedtime; another long embrace, another anchoring presence. By the next morning all of my chickadees had flown to be with me. My heart swelled. Tears flowed. Toto jumped for joy.

When the rabbi arrived, we gathered in the living room to tell him about Dan. Each of us chimed in:

"He adored his grandchildren."

"He had a talent for…"

"Graduated magna cum laude. "

"He loved the water, deep sea fishing… "

Later that morning, at the memorial service, the rabbi, perched on my mother's country French chair facing into our living room, recounted the stories and led us through the comforting, life-affirming ritual of the Mourner's Kaddish. I thought about all the religious rituals Dan and I had shared to celebrate life passages: from our wedding to the naming ceremonies for our children, their Bar and Bat Mitzvahs, graduations and weddings, and a generation later, their children's rites of passage. How we'd leaned on each other as our parents passed from this world, and now here I was, supported by our children as we mourned his passing. I looked around—my husband's world had shrunk to these few faces. No old friends and neighbors, no colleagues in our small gathering—but it felt right. I sat between Jenna and Jake on the floral-print sectional, across from the bay window. We'd pulled up dining room chairs for Kay and her husband, Joe. Sandra and Ron sat at right angles to us, facing the fireplace wall, the mirror draped in black. Behind them? An abstract oil painting of a girl feeding pigeons, the first painting Dan and I bought, from the artist's studio in Sarasota on a visit to my mom. Could that really have been forty-two years ago?

After the brief service, I walked the rabbi to the door. "Thank you. You've been so helpful."

I meant it. I'd been comforted by his presence, his tribute to Dan, and the familiar words of our tradition he'd offered.

Somehow the glass-and-brass dining room table had filled with platters of cold cuts, potato salad, coleslaw and pastries, but the person who'd have loaded his plate with those favorites was missing. Dan's comfort food comforted us. While spreading some chopped liver on a slice of rye bread, I pictured all the delis Dan and I'd enjoyed in Chicago, Houston, and other places during our travels.

At some point Ron had answered the door and returned with flowers from my coworkers. Another delivery brought an Edible Arrangements fruit bouquet.

"Who's that from?"

"The card says, 'Deepest sympathy, Donna and Tom.'" My personal trainer and her husband.

My hairdresser, Dan's too, had popped in with a plate of Korean pastries she'd made. "I'm so sorry," she whispered as we hugged, "I'm not staying, you be with your family."

I appreciated these kindnesses but was keenly aware that they weren't from old, close friends like those we'd left behind in Houston, or friends from childhood through college days.

After lunch Sandra had said, "Mom, there's a blizzard coming. If we don't leave tonight, we may not get out for days. We asked our neighbor to keep the kids for one night."

So, the first child who'd arrived in my life was the first to hug me goodbye. She'd been closest to her dad, and his champion when he'd tried my patience.

All those arguments we'd had, always about the same thing:

Me: "Two double cheeseburgers and fries? What are you thinking? How can you take all those heart meds at breakfast and chow down on that cholesterol combo for lunch?"

Dan: "So I'll drop dead."

"What if you don't go that way? I'm afraid you'll have a stroke like your dad. Don't expect me to feed you and change your diapers."

Well, he'd done it his way. Alive one minute, gone the next.

The weather forecasts were accurate. Dubbed 'Snowpocalypse' by the media, the blizzard covered the house and driveway with sixteen inches of snow.

That night, emotionally drained and numb, I was sitting in the living room looking through family albums with Jake and Jenna when it hit me. I turned to them and said, "Oh. I'm a widow."

Jake replied, drawing out each syllable as support groups do, "Hi, Barbara."

We could still laugh!

The next morning, Jenna, so quietly reassuring and unfailingly thoughtful, said, "Tell me what you want in the obituary, and where to send it. I'll take care of it when I get home."

"Thanks, sweetheart. Let's send one to his hometown paper, and to the Jewish newspapers here and in Houston." Then I realized: When I'd spoken to the rabbi, instead of Dan's alma mater, I'd named a different university in the same city… *Why would I have done that? I must've been in shock.*

As we sat at the breakfast table listing the key facts for the death notice, with the correct name of his university, it struck me how little of a life story those lines would tell.

As soon as the roads were clear, Jenna went back to the funeral home to identify Dan's body. I was and always will be grateful to her for that.

Most of a week went by before Jenna flew back to her family and her life. Clinging to each other as she left, I choked out, "Thanks for everything. I love you."

Lanky, laid-back Jake, single and ten years younger than his sisters, stayed with me for the first two weeks. We carried on, as we had a lifetime ago after his sisters left for college. He answered the phone one day.

"Mom, that was the funeral home. Dad's ashes are ready. The roads are clear now. I'll go. Give me that vase you want to use."

So I was spared a return visit to that house of death.

We placed the pewter vase containing Dan's ashes in the dining room next to the tall, flickering memorial candle on the glass-and-brass étagère. My first encounter with cremation, although it will be my choice too.

"I know this makes more sense than a burial," I'd told my cousin when she called, "but every time I see that vase, I feel queasy."

Jake and I passed the time playing Scrabble and watching old movies. At dinner one night, he announced: "Before I go back, I'm going to sell Dad's car and yours. We need to get you a reliable car."

One morning, his lean, six-foot frame sprawled out on the sofa with his laptop, he said, "I found a Prius with nineteen thousand miles that sounds great. I'm calling to see if they'll come down on the price."

"You can't negotiate on the phone."

"Watch me!"

Sure enough, they met Jake's price. We went to pick up the car I'm still driving. Jake handled everything. Days later he flew home, taking that pewter vase with him, with plans to take it across the country to Sandra's and drive with her to a spot on the North Carolina coast.

"He loved it there, Mom," Sandra reminded me. "We'll choose a beautiful day."

Did I feel guilty putting that task on them? Do I still? Not as much as I think I should.

When the roads cleared, Jake left.

Since the roads were impassable while I was sitting Shiva, the traditional week of mourning, that week passed before anyone could come to see me. The following week I received one visitor—someone I knew from work. One. Not the constant flow of familiar, caring faces of another time, other places, bearing briskets and casseroles, chatting about anything, just there.

Alone. Numb. Staring at the blank slate of my tomorrows. Wondering, "What now?"

A line from a Mary Oliver poem kept going through my mind: "Tell me, what is it you plan to do with your one wild and precious life?"

The Mourning Fog

As if to dull the pain, I learned that Mother Nature casts a fog over the mind of the recently bereaved. Faced with a long list of tedious tasks to complete during the days and weeks after Dan's death, I'd sit in a ratty old sweater and baggy, saggy jeans writing thank-you notes for floral arrangements, baked goods, and donations; notifying Social Security, closing joint bank accounts and completing paperwork to reopen them in my name; canceling credit cards; and sending countless death certificates to notify insurance companies, financial institutions, and governmental agencies to announce that, yes, the man I'd shared my life with for forty-two years was dead. Then, suddenly, I'd find myself unable to think clearly, to produce an answer to a mundane question, like "how long have you lived at this address?" That fog would descend and disappear at random times; like the unbidden, unwelcome status of widowhood, the fog was something that happened to me, over which I had no control. It was as if an opaque curtain had dropped, making my conscious mind inaccessible.

I wouldn't have known that others experience this mental murkiness if I hadn't joined a grief recovery group. And I wouldn't have joined at all without the gentle suggestion of my primary care doctor.

Like reaching out to clutch a sapling while sliding down a muddy slope, I followed my doctor's advice. A grief group? *Oh*, I'd thought—*maybe worth a try, but would it help?*

♥♥

A week later, I walked into a standard-issue classroom in a church annex and took a seat at a long fake-wood table with metal legs. Looking around, I saw faces of all ages; nine subdued, unsmiling women. At the head of the table a slim, grey-haired woman in a modest long-sleeved blouse and tailored skirt welcomed us and passed out some literature.

"Let's begin with introductions," she said, and started with herself. "I'm Charlene Wilkins," she said, in a soft, gentle voice. "When my husband died years ago, I found much-needed support from a grief group at my church. So, when I moved to this area, I started this program to create a healing space for new widows and widowers."

Then Charlotte asked us to introduce ourselves and describe the loss that had brought us here.

As we went around the table, it felt odd to identify myself by name and bereavement circumstances: "Hi, I'm Barbara, my husband died suddenly last month. His heart stopped."

In halting voices, tears breaking through, we went around the table, each of us trying to distill into a few words the circumstances and life-altering impact of losing the spouses with whom our lives were interwoven. Losing the sole owners of so many once-shared memories. As I looked around, I saw the truth of that old saying: death is the great leveler. It struck me that ordinarily the members of this group would never have crossed paths.

What a mix: Teresa, a hairdresser in her thirties whose husband had succumbed to kidney disease; Pam, a composed but clearly heartbroken mother of teenage boys, whose husband had suffered a fatal heart attack; Suzanne, a smartly clad woman in her twenties whose husband, a community leader and aspiring political candidate, had lost a battle with cancer, leaving her with two young children; Donna, a heavyset black woman, recently retired from the phone company, who'd been enjoying long-awaited cross-country travel, rallies, and social gatherings with her husband and their Harley Owners Club chapter until a stroke claimed his life.

I asked Donna, "What were some of your favorite trips?"

Her face came alive when she said, "Oh, we had a great time in New Orleans, and enjoyed mint juleps with other clubs at the Derby—what a hoot!"

While my brain strained to picture this silver-haired, matronly woman as a helmeted, leather-clad biker, my heart hurt when she said, "I can't drive the Harley, but our social life revolved around that club. Will I lose those friends?"

As a recent transplant to the DC area, I sorely missed the support and company of old friends. I wondered: was she going to suffer the same social isolation?

❧

Every Wednesday evening for nine weeks, emotions raw, each of us recounted our struggles: to assume both parenting roles, run households alone, or summon the energy to get up each day. The handouts we received at those meetings ran the gamut from *Falling Apart*, *Steps to Survival*, and this excerpt from *The Journey Through Grief* by Alan Wolfert, Ph.D., (Routledge; August 1, 1997):

> *Others have been where you are now, have moved through the phases of grieving that are new to you but not new at all, and have emerged changed, but whole.*

In the first throes of grief, we couldn't imagine the end of that journey, but it was some comfort to know that we were expected, even likely, to follow a well-traveled path.

Teresa, the slim, sweet hairdresser with shoulder-grazing auburn curls told us she'd had to close her home business to comply with neighborhood restrictions. She'd been visiting salons to find one that she could afford to join and that might be a good fit. She seemed lost, unable to make that decision, still reeling from the loss of her husband. Patty, on bereavement leave from her government job, had turned to her priest for solace; Suzanne, the young suburban housewife, overwhelmed by her own loss, struggled to help her bewildered children; Donna, the Harley rider, spent each day eating comfort food and watching TV. And I, recently relocated, newly retired, with no professional calling or colleagues, no family nearby, and no social network suddenly, after all those years of marriage, found myself alone. How would I fill the blank space?

As the weeks went by, with guidance from the group leader aided by handouts—practical and philosophical—we'd go around the table sharing how we were getting along. Some of the issues we heard were unique to one person, but ears perked up, pens came out, when Patty mentioned, "I found a great handyman."

One day I mentioned, "I'll be writing a note or working at the computer and suddenly I'll lose my concentration, as if a 'service interrupted' sign had popped up on my brain."

"That happens to me, too," someone said, "in the middle of a conversation I'll lose my train of thought."

Then one after another joined the chorus. Puzzled, I turned to Google for an explanation, typing 'brain fog following bereavement'. Immediately articles captioned 'Widow Fog', or 'Grief Brain' popped up. Oh. Turns out that intense grief triggers a chemical reaction throughout your body and brain that often lasts about three months. And the amygdala gets into the act, causing too much or too little sleep. I'd fall asleep easily but wake in the wee small hours and stay awake. A visit to my doctor proved to be a godsend. A caring, knowledgeable woman whose help proved to be invaluable, she prescribed a tiny dose of a powerful drug to help me get the rest I needed and connected me to a psychologist who helped me cope with a myriad of practical, social, and emotional issues. A mature woman, she officed in an inviting, earth-tone-furnished room on the lower level of her home on a quiet street in northwest D.C. During weekly meetings over the next several months she gave me specific suggestions, all of which proved helpful as I sought to revive my spirit and break my solitude:

"You need to be up and dressed each morning by 9 a.m."

By 9 a.m.? Why? I have nowhere to be, no one's expecting me. Oh well. She's the pro, I'm new at this. Might as well try it.

Each time we met, she offered specific suggestions:

"There's a lunch-and-learn group at the civic center you might enjoy. And give your library's book club a try. Get out of the house every day, even for errands."

From the first week on, my children took on new roles:

Jenna told me, "I brought copies of Dad's magazines home to Arizona so I can cancel his subscriptions."

Sandra, closer to her father than her siblings, said, "When Jake visits me, we'll scatter Dad's ashes at Topsail Beach on the Outer Banks. Dad loved that spot."

I started checking in with Jenna each morning, so someone would know that I'm alive and well. When tackling matters that Dan used to handle, I'd 'use a lifeline' to call my children for help. Dan died in December. Weeks later I called Jenna to say, "They're predicting a hard freeze tomorrow night, the weather alert advised covering outside faucets. I have no idea how to do that."

She'd left winters behind when she and her family moved to Phoenix, but she knew how to handle cold weather: "Home Depot has foam covers for the faucets. Ask someone there how to put them on."

So I ventured into the unfamiliar terrain of Home Depot, and sure enough, a kind employee not only showed me where to find the covers but patiently explained how to attach them. That evening, dressed in triple layers of my warmest clothes and knee-high snow boots, I tramped through the snowdrifts looking for outside faucets, found them, fumbled around, and eventually attached the odd-shaped gizmos. I felt like I was five years old, proud to say, "I did it myself!"

Day after day, month after month, I slogged through unfamiliar tasks, setting up utility accounts in my name (a multi-year battle with the electric company), canceling insurance policies in both names, working with an agent to choose the coverage I'd need for policies in my name, ordering a memorial plaque at the Houston congregation where we'd raised our family. Adding Dan's plaque to our parents'—who expects they'll have to do that?

"I'm drowning in paperwork, battling bureaucrats every day," I told Sandra.

"Don't try to tackle everything at once," she said. "Figure out what needs attention right now. Set the rest aside."

Luckily, I had the means to maintain my lifestyle and stay in the house, but that meant dealing with home maintenance, lawn care and such—ugh. I kept the same contractors that Dan had engaged. They knew more about what needed doing than I did.

After two years, I got around to changing my will. We didn't have a lawyer. A member of my grief group recommended an estate-planning specialist; she gently guided me through the process.

Some post-bereavement tasks had no urgency, like sorting through Dan's clothes, tennis, and fishing equipment, and 'stuff'. In time, I gave Jake his dad's cashmere overcoat and sent my grandson the well-used but long-idled Prince tennis racket.

My trickiest project, finding a home for Dan's fishing tackle, dragged on—checking the value of each rod and reel, posting ads on local listservs—trying but failing to find a charity that could use them. That gear held his happiest memories, out in the Atlantic battling swordfish with his dad, landing a fifty-pound white marlin on our Bermuda honeymoon, and catching red snapper in the Gulf of Mexico off Galveston on weekend outings with his best buddy. Out in the elements he was in his element, breaking the silence of the natural beauty around him to cry, "I've got one on! It's a keeper!"

Those rods and reels trace the arc of our marriage, hunting bonefish in a flat-bottomed skiff in the Florida Keys, dock-fishing at night in Sarasota, frying up a trout our daughter caught in a Colorado stream, squealing with delight, her daddy coaching her, "let it run; now pull it in slowly."

No wonder I kept those rods and reels, hooks, sinkers, and fishing line long after he was gone. Other widows must have similar untouchables—books covered with handwritten notes, or cameras, lenses, and scuffed-up leather camera cases. Letting go of those memory-laden objects meant letting go of a lifetime together. The fishing gear has taken up permanent residence in my basement.

For me and for each of us in our bereavement group, the learning curve was steep; the decisions challenging; the tasks tedious. My to-do-list was long, with progress slowed by those unpredictable mental lapses. It didn't help to have a veil fall over my thought processes again and again. Or did it? Maybe that was a blessing in disguise, dulling the pain, diminishing the discomfort during a period of devastating disorientation.

In Sickness and In Health

To love someone long-term is to attend a thousand funerals of the people they used to be… We so badly want the people we love to get their spark back when it burns out…
But it is not our job to hold anyone accountable for the people they used to be. It is our job to travel with them…and to honor what emerges along the way.

Heidi Priebe, author

I thought we'd grow old together.

We didn't. We were the same age, but Dan grew old decades before I did. At mid-life, Dan's career ended. Suddenly. Without warning. Despite years of glowing performance reviews and promotions, his Big 8 accounting firm declined to make him a partner. The partnership was a tight-knit group of men whose families belonged to the same churches and socialized together at an elite country club that did not admit Jews. Dan and our family wouldn't fit into the partnership, so that was the end of the road for Dan with that company or any of its Big 6 counterparts. We lived in Houston; no small or medium-sized accounting firms needed Dan's experience auditing Fortune 500 companies. So, his career dead-ended, his self-esteem tanked, and his zest for life evaporated. A devastating blow to this lifelong super-achiever.

At first he tried to hang out a shingle for a private practice, sharing offices with two other former Arthur Andersen CPAs. But his experience was with multinational corporations; he had little to offer small business owners or individuals. In time he moved his desk to a handsome home office we created for him, but he had no network to tap; there were no calls for his services.

Meanwhile my career was zooming along; I outperformed my global counterparts and won entry into the 'crème de la crème' of the leaders in my field.

In time Dan had to give up on finding work. Diving into the 'Mr. Mom' role, he took pride in mastering mundane household tasks like separating colors and whites and developing systematic approaches to grocery shopping. In the years before they went off to college, the girls helped with their younger brother, meeting his bus after school and driving his carpools once they had licenses. When they went off to out-of-state colleges, Jake was in junior high, then high school. He needed Dan's help with meals, homework and such much less after his sixteenth birthday, when he could drive himself. Two years later, with his high school diploma in hand, Jake left for Los Angeles to pursue a screenwriting career. All of our chickadees had left the nest. Dan had no work, no daily parenting responsibilities, no purpose—just an occasional tennis game or weekend fishing trip to fill his days.

Just as his mother had before him, in his mid-fifties Dan withdrew from life, swathed in sadness. And, as his self-esteem shrunk, his waistline expanded. Over many years, his broad muscular chest sunk into a cummerbund of excessive weight, and his once trim one-hundred-and-eighty-pound physique dissolved into three-hundred-and-fifty pounds of flab. We were the same age, but by age sixty Dan looked and acted like an old man. Instead of REI or Macy's, this once virile, athletic outdoorsman shopped at Big-and-Tall stores. At restaurants he'd request a table because he couldn't squeeze into a booth; on planes he needed a seat belt extender. At movie theaters we'd take three seats, leaving one between us, because his body spilled over the bounds of a single seat. At parties, where once he'd circulated, surveyed the buffet, then made his choices, now he'd sit in one spot the whole evening chatting with old friends, relying on me to bring him a plate.

Dan didn't seem bothered that he was sidelined while his friends were enjoying professional and material success. The generosity of his wealthy parents proved to be a double-edged sword, providing financial security for our family, promising significant bequests in their wills, but obviating Dan's need to earn a living.

For years after the career-ending blow, Dan tried to put a cheerful face on his situation. He enjoyed deep-sea fishing with his best buddy, kibitzed with his tennis partners after each game at our neighborhood swim club, and served as treasurer on the club's board of directors. At one point the board offered him a paid job as their accountant.

"Oh," I thought, "tapping his skills and earning some money would give him an ego boost."

But no, he declined; a far cry from auditing giant corporations, he viewed that job with disdain. He seemed to be content with his life as a retired, at-home dad. But a current of anger was never far from the surface, ready to flare when one of the children sassed him or acted out. He rarely lashed out at me.

Dan and I shared a long history and memories from college and beyond. We'd been married seventeen years when his career ended. As for me, a longtime stay-at-home mom, when our daughters reached school age, I became a volunteer leader—at the local, regional, then national levels—of an organization serving low-income youth. Then, in my role as a volunteer leader, I picked up the threads of my early career and launched a project to address adult literacy in Houston.

The project gained traction, won the mayor's attention, and two years later the mayor and city council created a mayoral literacy initiative, naming me the executive director.

Did they ask me first? No. But did I want the job? Oh, yes. Dan was floundering, but he'd settled into his routine at home, and we needed the income and benefits I'd receive. So we switched roles; he held the fort at home and I headed downtown. I was on a high, flexing my intellectual muscles, heady with joy to be back in the workforce, engaged in creating and leading an exciting new initiative.

Suddenly, in our mid-forties, I was energized, engaged and excited about my work, putting high heels on and driving to the heart of downtown each day. I was rarin' to go, having channeled my drive and leadership skills into volunteer roles for too long. I was thrilled to have an income, recognition, and a job that gave me the chance to offer low-literate adults a path to and beyond a high school equivalency diploma.

One of the first things I did, once I had money of my own? Purchase a life insurance policy for our son equal to the trust funds my in-laws' estates had established for our daughters. Suddenly I had a start toward financial independence—pretty heady stuff after twenty years as a hausfrau.

What was it like to be given the reins of this mayoral commission, with the mission to implement the plan for the citywide literacy initiative I'd envisioned? I welcomed the opportunity. I credit my dad for that because, even though his aspirations for me were traditional, he'd always nurtured my ideas and delighted in and shared my proclivity for challenging convention. Unwittingly—since the only safe route Dad saw for me was to become an at-home wife and mother—his admiration encouraged me to imagine, grasp, and savor nontraditional professional opportunities.

Dan remembered how I'd loved my War on Poverty and volunteer leadership jobs. As I encountered financial management issues in my new position, he was quick to offer helpful advice. But while he tried to put a good face on his role as an at-home dad, I saw that he was depressed, discouraged, and drowning in the drudgery of domestic chores.

Caught in a self-defeating cycle, Dan's hopelessness kept him from seeking help. He became irritable, quick to scold the children or snap at me. Once, when his frustration erupted, he punched a hole in our family room wall. The children and I began to tread lightly around him.

For the first time in our married lives, I thought about divorce. But there were many factors that ruled against it. Our three children were flourishing in gifted programs at excellent local schools, living in a safe neighborhood, carpooling with the kids they'd grown up with, enjoying a house with a swimming pool and rooms of their own. I had no savings of my own; Dan's trust fund provided our financial security. On my salary—even with alimony—I'd have had to uproot the children, drastically diminish their material comforts, and jeopardize their educational progress.

Our children were thriving. I couldn't do that to them.

Then miraculously, Dan agreed to couples counseling. At our first session the therapist asked Dan, "What brings you here today?" I inhaled hope, then exhaled despair when his once-over-lightly reply revealed he wouldn't, or couldn't, acknowledge the chasm between us. The therapy began and ended that day.

My hopes revived when Dan decided to try gastric bypass surgery. But before accepting him as a patient, the surgeon challenged him: "Come back in one month. Between now and then, restrict your diet to the small amounts required of post-surgical patients. If you can do that, we'll schedule your surgery."

Dan lost twenty-five pounds that month. So, he decided, "I don't need the surgery. I can do this."

Well, he couldn't.

I tried to be supportive of Dan without diverting my energies and attention from our children's needs or my career. As for our relationship, the glue that held us together was all that we'd shared: our flaming college romance, blissful newlywed years, private jokes, parenting, celebrating milestones, helping—then losing—our parents, and much more. Missing way too soon: our once-vibrant sexual intimacy.

We were in our fifties when I applied for the enticing opportunity to direct the U.S. program of Ashoka, a global network of social entrepreneurs. My shot in the dark application yielded an offer for a dream job. We had to move to D.C., but we were empty nesters, and our daughter Jenna lived there, so Dan was all in. I jumped at the chance to say yes.

As my best friend in Houston hugged me goodbye, she said, "I hope they know that change is coming."

I started that job in December 2003. During my tenure the U.S. program flourished. I gained national attention. Pretty heady stuff.

After work I'd share the ins and outs of my day with Dan:

"I'm going to Alaska to meet a candidate. All on the company's dime!"

"Our summer intern's a godsend. I wish she could stay."

Like a pet savoring table scraps, Dan experienced my work vicariously, sympathizing when I struggled, celebrating when I succeeded. Sometimes he'd help me prepare an annual budget or suggest ways to handle a personnel issue. He was wonderfully supportive in that way. But I remembered, sorrowfully, that it had once been Dan who had projects to discuss and success after success to celebrate.

Dan and I had shared so much. After an eight-year on-and-off courtship (starting my first week of college) we'd begun married life on a high, welcomed two little girls in two years, then our son ten years later. So many memories: crisscrossing the country in a motorhome toting three kids; marking life's passages with family; celebrating children's achievements; tending to, then losing our parents; and much more. True, I'd thought about leaving him when I was in my prime and he'd retreated from life, but after the children left the nest, I'd thrown myself into work while Dan sat at home; I didn't have the energy or the heart to consider divorce.

Eventually Dan's weight taxed his body's resiliency. One afternoon we were chatting when I realized Dan's comments didn't make sense; he was speaking gibberish. I called 911. Alarm bells rang in my heart and in the ambulance that raced him to the hospital. As I sat in the emergency room waiting area, I wondered how my life was about to change. But the next morning when I entered the ICU, Dan was sitting up, chatting with the nurse while he ate breakfast. The doctor released him that afternoon, but said, "I want to see you in my office next week."

"Doctor," I said, standing out of Dan's earshot, "he suffers from depression. Please help him."

But after Dan's follow-up visit, the doctor told me, "He has to be more proactive to benefit from psychotherapy." Argh. I was crestfallen. And angry. 'Proactive' and 'depressed' are mutually exclusive. That guy must've slept through his psych courses.

Sometimes affable, sometimes surly, Dan sat out the years that followed, buoyed only by family visits, first with daughter Sandra's little girls, then Jenna's baby, our first grandson. Oh, how Dan loved having that little guy nearby!

In photos of Dan during the grandkids' early years his face radiated joy. But in all the photos, the little ones are on his lap. He couldn't get down on the floor to play with them.

One evening Dan called out to me, "I can't breathe." Another sirens-blaring ride to the hospital, followed by regular visits to a cardiologist, and a new course of medication.

Always thinking of us, Sandra called. "Dad," she said, "I ordered a weight loss program for you. They'll deliver calorie-controlled meals and snacks. Worth a try!"

My hopes rose, only to be dashed again. Dan wouldn't—or couldn't—stick to a weight loss program. He couldn't stay away from drive-through diet-busters. Even after a two-week hospitalization that left him so weakened he needed a week at a rehab hospital, he began seeing a cardiologist who prescribed medications and lifestyle changes.

I came home one day to find him polishing off a triple Whopper with fries. "How can you see the cardiologist, take your heart meds, then eat like this?"

"Oh, shut it. So I'll die."

"It's not just about you," I snapped back. "What about me?"

Trapped in the depths of his disease, he couldn't rally for his own sake, much less mine. Something as simple as dining out at a restaurant ended on a sour note for me when, as we made our way to the exit, Dan put his hand on other diners' tables as a prop because his legs could no longer bear his weight. I was so embarrassed, imagining how offensive it would be to have a stranger use my dinner table as a hand-rest.

Maybe, as author Heidi Priebe believes, I should have "honored the person he'd become." But Dan's choices had not only diminished his but also my life. And no halo graces my head.

In December 2009, at age sixty-eight, Dan's overburdened heart gave out. And I became a widow.

Identity Loss

I retired by accident. Six months before Dan died, I decided to leave the job in Washington that I'd loved and derived great satisfaction from: supporting the success of individuals offering breakthrough solutions to intractable social problems like homelessness, elder care, or climate change. Their programs had fueled my imagination. Working closely with these remarkable people had enriched my life. Still, it was time to move on. I'd grown weary of overperforming while understaffed. A colleague advised me: "Set your intention. Tell me a date certain, and I'll support you."

It took a while, but I made the leap. In November I told her, "After the first of the year."

Serendipitously, within a month, Ella, one of the candidates I'd guided to lifetime election to the Ashoka fellowship, had approached me: "We're ready to replicate our model nationwide," she'd told me. "I've talked to our board and staff; we want you to lead that effort."

"I'm intrigued," I said, "but you're in the Midwest. I don't want to relocate."

"You wouldn't have to! You can work remotely. We'll cover your travel expenses for meetings and site visits."

For years I'd spent two hours a day commuting to and from work. Here was a chance to work from home and help bring this life-enhancing multi-generational program to communities throughout the country. Picture a quiet neighborhood of two-story single-family homes. On one side of the street, senior residents live in rent-reduced apartments; on the other, families in the process of adopting foster children dwell in houses. The seniors serve as surrogate grandparents, caring for preschoolers, helping school-age children with homework, and providing after school care—so their mid-life neighbors can hold full-time jobs. Brilliant.

What a great career-capping opportunity!

"You'd be the Director of Strategic Initiatives, earning the same salary I do," she offered.

That did it. For the first time I'd be earning a six-figure salary.

"Let's do it!"

In January I turned in my keys to the office and walked away, feeling great about what I'd accomplished, but weary of pushing myself to meet one unreasonable goal after another. Weeks later, I flew to the university for a team meeting. I'd met Ella's small, collegial team when I'd made a site visit during her candidacy. But I'd never worked with tenured academics before. On this visit I saw them in a new light.

"I've been thinking," one team member said. "Maybe we should tweak the model. What if we expand the application process to include employment histories?"

Another said, "Yes, let's revise the white paper."

Uh-oh. They were still debating changes to the program I'd been hired to replicate.

To them, the intergenerational community they'd created was still a theoretical experiment. But social entrepreneurs learn by doing, not by publishing papers in academic journals.

Chastened, I still hoped we could finalize the 'blueprint' so other communities could replicate it. But after six months it was clear: they weren't ready to do that. They couldn't get past endless debates about how to improve the program. Crestfallen, bitterly disappointed, I gave my notice.

Now what? Unemployed. At home. No work to excite my imagination, no more problem-solving excursions that revved my intellectual engines. What a let-down! After posting my resume on non-profit job sites, I began doing what unemployed professionals do: develop a consulting practice.

"I'm calling it 'Achieving Change Together'," I told a former colleague. "Do you know someone who can design a logo?"

She did. With that done I began writing the copy for a website and working with a web designer. That kept me busy for months, right through the fall.

"I'll wait till January to promote it," I'd told the web designer. "Nothing happens in December."

Well, something did. That one day in mid-December, Dan died.

January came and went. And the next month, and the next. I lacked the energy or enthusiasm needed to launch a consulting practice. I turned to a book that had helped me in the past, *The Way of Transition: Embracing Life's Most Difficult Moments*. Author William Bridges describes transition as "the inner reorientation and self-redefinition that you have to go through." He explains that endings and losses are signaled by one of several experiences:

> - a sudden and unexpected event that destroys the old life that made you feel like yourself (my husband's death)
> - the 'drying up' of a situation or a relationship that once felt vital and alive (my career)
> - an activity that has always gone well before, suddenly and unexpectedly goes badly (my work)
> - a person or an organization that you have always trusted proves to be untrustworthy and your whole sense of reality comes apart (the colleague who offered me that no-win job)

Oh yeah. There was no rushing the process. Bridges also said that it was common to feel depressed, defeated, and confused when endings happen. Although my consulting practice was ready to launch, after the shock of Dan's death I lacked the oomph to beat the bushes for prospective clients or to focus on the work when I landed one. After a few consulting gigs, still searching—not finding—a perfect fit for a woman of sixty-eight with an interesting but atypical resumé, I gave up the chase.

Like many turning points in my unplanned life, I wound up where I hadn't expected: widowed and retired. It hurt. That incredible one-two punch almost had me down for the count. There seemed to be a sign over these situations: No exit.

> *When grieving recedes, one wants to see a path forward. In time, through trial and error, that path will emerge, reflecting one's new outlook and preferences.*

Remembering

My husband loved nature. At age five a bout with pneumonia confined him to quarters, too frail to play with other children at Fort Lewis, Washington, the army base where he and his mom waited for the return of his dad, a medical doctor serving in London during WWII. Happily, the five-year-old spent most of his days at a pristine mountain lake. Feet dangling from a dock, he entertained himself by feeding ducks, skipping stones, and watching wildlife. That was the start of his love affair with water and the outdoor world.

Back home in Michigan, summer escapes to a lakeside cottage found him in or on the water for hours on end. Throughout childhood, his growth was measured, not by notches on a wall, but by increased stamina, strength, and speed in competitive swimming as he moved from one age group to the next. Every winter, his family headed to Miami, where he discovered the sea. The little boy, enthralled by the sights and sounds of a quiet lake, rejoiced at being out on the open water. From adolescence through the prime of life, the sea was his solace, game fish his challenge, water his element. Poet Ted Hughes understood: "Fishing provides that connection with the whole living world. It gives you the opportunity of being totally immersed, turning back into yourself in a good way."

In adolescence the once frail boy led the swim team to state championships. His summer job during college? Waterfront camp counselor in Michigan's scenic Upper Peninsula.

College brought us together, too young to be serious but too smitten to forget. Eight years later we married, and…wait for it…set sail for Bermuda, a fishing paradise. On the last day of our honeymoon, his dream came true. The charter boat captain shouted, "He caught a forty-five-pound Wahoo!" "He just landed a white marlin!" "Another Wahoo!" My new husband was having the time of his life. His bride? From my cot in the cabin I muttered feeble "yahoos" between waves of nausea. I sensed then that Mother Nature would be the other woman in *our* romance.

Our first home, a condo high above Lake Michigan, was literally at the water's edge. A guardrail stood between our front door and the water. From our high-rise aerie we watched sun and storms transform the sky, and summer regattas dot the lake with color.

Fast forward ten years to Houston, two children, a challenging career, and a hefty mortgage. Plus untamed backyard vegetation demanding attention that was no fun at all. No match for the Gulf of Mexico that promised my husband action he hadn't seen since our honeymoon.

The broiling sun and roiling sea held no attraction for me. I gladly ceded that arena—and our weekends—to my rival. Unfazed by the heat and the motion, for him the watching and waiting was like foreplay. And when he cried, "I've got one on!" the ensuing dance with a wet and wild partner rarely failed to satisfy. These sweaty encounters lasted longer than lovemaking, testing his strength and proving his manhood by classic measure. The longed-for trophy fish did not surface often, but the chance that she might, kept tensions high.

Hemingway knew. *In the Old Man and the Sea* he said the fisherman always thought of the sea "as feminine and as something that gave or withheld great favours." Still, I was the flesh-and-blood woman my man came home to with his catch, photos and graphic stories that captured—and embellished on—the rapture. What other extra-marital escapade comes with bragging rights?

Those were his glory days. In time the ocean gave way to a backyard pool and hot tub. No pool got more loving attention than ours. Filling the skimmer with leaves and debris made his time outdoors purposeful, rewarded by frequent, refreshing dips. Each lap reminded his aging muscles of the rhythm and flow of the stroke that once won championships.

At dawn and dusk the hot tub was his haven—perfect for spotting birds, frogs and whatever creatures happened by. From air-conditioned comfort I listened for his whistle, summoning me to see an uncommon specimen or spectacular sunset.

With an empty nest, and a gold watch, we retired to the north, exchanging the pool for a heavily wooded yard. Romance with me and with the sea competed for space in his memory.

Limited again by frailty as he was in childhood, his easy chair became a vantage point for viewing birds, deer, and an occasional fox. His life, and his love affair with nature, had come full circle.

Now he is gone. I sit in that chair, hearing him call with the excitement of a five year old: "Baby deer! Hurry!" But it's the chipmunk whose rare appearance brings memories flooding back, of a man who patiently watched for and found pleasure in nature's bounty, mundane or exotic. The ducks of his childhood delighted him as much as the white marlin of his prime. A tiny chipmunk brightened his last days. A gift from my old rival, that chipmunk brings him back to me.

Phase Two

Reaching Out/Learning

At age sixty-eight, after a lifetime of a calendar filled by school, work, marriage, family, and community commitments, I found myself woefully unprepared for the vast vista and uncharted terrain of widowhood. Now, for several months after Dan's death, instead of checking the calendar to see where I had to show up, what I had to do, and what I had to prepare for children, spouse, and others, my days began with wonder: How will I fill the hours? Sitting in the tweed-covered armchair passed down to me by my dad, I struggled to come up with a plan for the day.

The tasks ahead were daunting—to find friends, purposeful engagement, and connect to community—more urgent now that I no longer had Dan's companionship. I knew I had to start somewhere, but how to begin?

Get Up, Get Dressed, Now What?

For years, Dan's declining health and resistance to treatment had kept me on high alert for a health event that could, and then did, prove fatal. But I was caught unaware for another, profound loss: my place in the global social-change community.

In one year, my identity had taken two jolting, life-changing hits: 'Married' became 'widowed'. 'Director, U.S. Program' became 'retired'. One long anticipated. The second unexpected and unwelcome. Still profoundly sad.

In the first years after those losses, unsettling emotions sat just beneath the surface, poised to pierce through my defenses or derail my progress. Sometimes I felt stuck—without purpose or direction. Without warning, I'd descend into an emotional morass of anger, fear, and sadness. Suddenly I'd rail against the unfairness of it all—*why had my life taken these two blows in quick succession? What now?*

Struggling to cope with the sudden shifts in my life, I couldn't begin to imagine myself with renewed enthusiasm for life. Meeting each new day with dull despair, I couldn't see a way that my circumstances could change.

I read about people moving through the stages of grief. I understood that I could, and would, move through this funk. But I couldn't imagine how. Slowly, with the help of counseling, my support group, and my own indefatigable spirit, I did carry on. Those deep disappointments that had taken up residence in my psyche eventually took a backseat to the forward thrust of my life.

I credit my therapist for this much-needed kick in the pants: "By 9 a.m. each morning you're up, dressed and ready for the day."

I followed that advice faithfully for the first few years, even though I often couldn't imagine, "Now what?"

Free time once seemed like a luxury. Now it was a challenge. So many questions that I alone had to consider: What would engage me socially, pique my curiosity, or apply my talents purposefully? How and where could I find answers? Instead of responding to demands from outside sources, I was free to pick and choose activities. Few priorities helped to order my life. There was no urgency to act and no penalty for procrastination. So I'd ask myself what I wanted to do, when I wanted to do it, and how important it was to do it at all.

୧୭

Dan's long decline had prepared me—to some extent—for losing him. But I was not prepared for the other, profound losses: meaningful, intellectually exciting work for me, and my place in the community of idealistic change agents.

I had to rely on demands from within to get up and get going—to muster up the energy to find opportunities to be useful, have fun, and live a purposeful life. With no spouse, children and colleagues vying for my time and attention, I looked for, found, and created new projects—but all of them were part-time: consulting, volunteering, 'doing lunch', traveling, joining affinity groups, and signing up for educational programs. Each week was different. But that hodge podge of people to see, things to do, and places to go beat the alternative hands down. Planning ahead—never my strong suit—was essential.

This took grit, internal fortitude, perseverance. Despite all efforts, some days I had nowhere to be, nothing to do. The phone didn't ring. When my Google calendar scolded, "You have no events scheduled today," I'd go to the grocery store, pick up a takeout meal—anything that promised a "Have a nice day" from a checkout clerk or a chance meeting with a neighbor.

That's when I'd get up, get dressed, and do *something* to appreciate the gift each day brought. It was a personal journey, but I wasn't alone. I felt I was traveling with unseen co-travelers.

No New Messages

"**S**tudy: Don't Be Lonely, It's Bad for You" warned Atlantic columnist Lindsay Abrams. To which I'd say, "Easier said than done." Abrams' column caught my attention: University of Chicago psychologists found that chronic loneliness shortens a person's life by fourteen percent, a greater risk than obesity. In fact, men and women sixty and older were forty-five percent more likely to die during the six-year study if they reported feeling lonely, isolated, or left out. Well, great. It was hard enough to exchange a full nest and hectic workplace for the solitary confinement of living and working alone as a home-based consultant. I ate right, exercised, and practiced meditation. Now failing to fill my social calendar threatened to reduce my life expectancy!

Since being widowed, building a new social circle had been Job No.1 for me. For the first few years I poured myself into that effort: I joined, participated, and networked. Several years after Dan died, one of those efforts, co-chairing a non-profit diversity initiative for the Women's Connection, an organization for women 'fifty and forward', yielded a challenging cross-cultural project with remarkable women I would not otherwise have met. For two years that work excited my interest. It even led to a new consulting engagement. Then the initiative's founder stepped down and the group opted for 'shared leadership' (read "death by committee"). I made a quick exit. But it left a big hole in my life. So once again, I had to try on new activities to find a good fit.

Most of my new acquaintances disappeared on the weekend and holidays. Married, with family in town, they had friends they'd made when their kids were toddlers. I complained to my therapist, "I'm always the one who initiates social plans." She didn't mince words: "Get used to it. You need them more than they need you."

I felt like a rainmaker in a dessert. Despite all my efforts to "get out there and connect," converting acquaintances to friends takes time. I wanted to skip the social chit chat and go right to personal, one-on-one encounters. But it doesn't work that way. It was try one group, give up on it, try another; declaring defeat wasn't an option; I had to find friends.

After a year of attending monthly meetings at the Washington Ethical Society, someone suggested meeting for lunch. Oh, I'd thought, if that's how long it takes to build social capital, I needed to find a group that offers a better return on investment. But since my calendar was bare, I stuck with it anyway, and eventually formed a book club with

Linda, someone I'd met there. Did we see each other outside of these groups? No. Younger than me, she worked full time, had a live-in boyfriend, and a full life.

I was excited to meet a woman at a meeting about—wait for it—aging. Sharply dressed, with a confident air, I thought she might be my kind of people. So I plunked myself down beside her. Turned out we not only had a similar professional background (which never happens) but many of the same colleagues! She suggested meeting for dinner the next Saturday.

"Great," I said. "I never have plans on weekend nights."

"Join the club," she replied.

Delighted to find a single woman with similar interests and weekend availability, we agreed to put another meeting on the calendar. But the date she suggested was three months away! I moved her from 'Promising' to 'Don't Bother' on my BFF candidates list.

If networking was an Olympic event, I'd be vying for a medal. I worked and worked on it. But years after the double whammy of losing my husband and leaving my job, I was still home alone more often than not. Long weekends, eagerly anticipated during my career, were now dreaded empty space on my calendar.

I'd tried lunch-and-learn programs, Meet-ups, and even Senior Centers (who came up with that name, a recent college grad?). One such Center advises: "The stronger your links with others, the longer you are likely to live." That rang true. But I was loathe to cross those thresholds. The county's recreation director admitted that, "For some, a Senior Center evokes images of tottering 'old' people." Ya think?

During my career I'd relied on phone and email to work with colleagues and constituents; now I'd have welcomed, but rarely enjoyed, face time with consulting clients. So I'd go out to see people at meetings, yoga classes, and more. No matter how many hours I'd been out and about, when I came home there was no need to check voice mail. My phone would tell the same tiresome story: "No new messages."

My calendar looked like some kind of board game with less than half of the squares filled in. With lots of planning, ingenuity, and determination, that was the best I could do.

Our mobile, greying society has created legions of people like me—suddenly single, too young to sideline, with no family or friends with shared memories nearby. Now that we know this condition is hazardous to our health, wellness gurus have their work cut out for them. So hey, Dr. Phil, you'd better get busy. In those years I wondered—and still wonder—what's the healthy, wholesome antidote to loneliness?

That year is imprinted in my psyche. Even after a lifetime of accomplishments, memories of that nine-year-old me, the new kid, would still have the power to evoke anxiety when I'd be about to meet new people. I may be a liberated woman, but as a widow, in my forays into new social situations I worried about what to wear and how I'd look. I'd talk about myself a little longer than I should, so the people I'd meet would know I'm someone special. Pity the person who'd ask, "What do you do?" They'd want a concise, clear answer, "I'm a … (fill in the blank—lawyer, teacher, etc.)." They'd get a paragraph or two about what I used to do and what I do now. I couldn't say, "I'm dabbling in this and that," for fear of being viewed as the stereotypical retiree, with nothing sufficiently tantalizing to invite a second question. I just couldn't leave it at "Hello." I still needed to make the encounter yield what that nine-year-old girl had sought: approval and acceptance.

My parents' dream came true when they built our house in the suburbs. They'd scrimped and saved for twenty years to realize that dream. Until I was nine, our family of four lived in a two-bedroom, one-bath, five-room apartment in a three-story walk-up on Chicago's north side. I shared a bedroom with my sister. Grandpa and Grandma were present in my daily life. Surrounded by love, life was predictable and secure. That security vanished when we moved.

My parents had spent every penny on the house, so no back-to-school shopping for me. At school my hand-me-down clothes shouted "New girl. Not one of us." The fourth-grade girls seemed like they were born and raised in suburbia. Rosy-cheeked, cheerful, clad in colorful, coordinated outfits—pleated plaid skirts, colorful matching sweaters—they were nothing like the kids I'd known. We'd worn Sears' specials—corduroy pants, flannel shirts and non-descript dresses with clunky oxfords—practical, long-lasting (sigh) and cheap. Style? For children's clothes? Never entered my mother's mind.

In the city, at recess, we went out to a concrete-covered area with a few squeaky wooden swings and a worn-out tether ball. A chain link fence kept kids in and passersby out. No grassy field, baseball diamond, organized sports or games. We played hopscotch (bring your own chalk). In my new school the girls played a game that looked a lot like baseball, but the pitcher rolled the ball and the "batter" kicked it. Before each game the pitcher rattled off the rules; it sounded like "ishkabibblegobbledygookhassenfefer, pitcher's hands out!" I couldn't understand a word, so I sat on the sidelines. Eventually I caught on, but when teams were formed, I remember standing there, watching and waiting, while every other name was called before mine.

Four years a widow, I felt like that fourth grader again, a lonely outsider. I'd grown weary of joining groups, taking classes, and doing more than most to 'get out there' to meet people. The people I'd meet had friends and family in town who'd keep their calendars full.

Day after day, from wake-up to bedtime, it was just me and my dog. So if I'd meet someone, I'd think: I hope you like me. If you can make room in your life for me, let's get together. Weekends are always good.

I've Lost That Special Feeling

My immigrant grandparents came from two countries, Russia and Germany, but one culture: Judaism. Their shared language? Yiddish. When they arrived in Chicago, they looked for and found an apartment within walking distance of a synagogue and kosher butcher. I grew up in that neighborhood, knowing almost by osmosis that I was part of an age-old religion and culture. Unlike today when congregations come in as many flavors as ice cream, everyone in our family, and all of our Jewish friends—including those my parents knew from childhood—belonged to the same synagogue. Familiar faces greeted us with hugs and kisses when we arrived at services. We'd linger afterward to chat. The rabbi knew each of us by name. We belonged.

Over the course of my long life, I've lived in several places, making temporary moves before settling down, putting down roots in one place, then another. Wherever I've lived, my

Jewish identity gave me entrée to a community where I'd find instant connections and shared experiences with the people I'd encounter.

But when Dan died, I had no social network. After moving from Houston to suburban D.C., I'd been immersed in a demanding job that left no time or energy for chatting up neighbors or joining a community organization. On weekends and holidays, I'd enjoy time with my daughter Jenna and her family. But Jenna had moved to Arizona just before my life, like an hourglass, had tipped upside down and started over. If I'd been a commodity, my marketing monikers would have changed from 'director' and 'Mrs.' to 'retiree' and 'Ms.' But as a widow trying to create a new social network, I had no way to communicate my status, to signal prospective friends, "Available now, weekdays and weekends." No, I had to sign up and show up over and over again to meet kindred spirits. After a long slog, I did. Still, something was missing: a home in a Jewish congregation.

When Dan and I moved from Chicago to Houston with two preschoolers, we asked the realtor, " Are there Jewish families in this neighborhood?"

Why was it important for us to ask? To gain a head start on connecting with kindred spirits. There's a comfort level we have that comes from a shared history, beliefs, and traditions—who else would include gefilte fish or chopped liver in a holiday menu? Judaism has been described as a religion, a race, a culture, and a nation... The *Judaism 101* website sums it up this way: "The Jewish people are best described as an extended family." So, when Dan and I moved to Houston, we'd enrolled our girls in the Jewish Community Center preschool and found friends among the parents of their playmates. Within a year we'd joined a congregation. In time our wider circle looked like a slice of the American pie, but our temple, rabbi, and our Jewish friends anchored our lives.

Why am I rambling on about all this? Because as a new widow, when I'd needed to find community, I began searching for a Jewish congregation.

In time I found a temple that seemed 'just my speed'—small, self-described as welcoming, with a silver-haired, portly rabbi who exchanged kisses and warm smiles with congregants.

"This could be my Jewish home," I'd thought, after attending services there; so I became a member and set about sampling some adult education classes, special interest, and social action groups. But with a heavy heart, in my fifth year of membership, I could count on one hand the members I knew by name.

Most temples post board members at the door to greet congregants before services, wishing them *"Shabbat Shalom"* on Friday night or Saturday morning, and *"Shanah Tovah,"* a good year, on high holidays. But as a new member, the first time I'd showed up for Rosh Hashanah services, and again the most recent time, four years later, I arrived and left without a single person speaking to me. Even in an adult education class, participants only spoke to people they knew. The same thing happened during outings with the seniors group. Then, when the rabbi and cantor who'd inspired my affiliation were fired and retired in quick succession, I gave up on that congregation. Another loss. I felt more alone than ever.

All my life I've had a religious home. From birth through adulthood I'd shared that home, not only with my immediate family but with my grandparents, aunts, uncles, and cousins, and with my parents' friends—people I called "Aunt" or "Uncle"—and then with my husband, our own children, relatives, and friends. At mid-life we'd loved having those gray-haired elders at the table, linking the generations. Now I'm the grandparent. I'm happiest when I "have ticket, can travel" to celebrate holidays or rites of passage with my children and theirs. At a time in my life when nostalgia flows through my psyche like blood through my veins, those infrequent visits haven't been enough for me. I've craved a congregation a little like *Cheers*, where at least some people would know my name. The disappointment I felt, sat in my chest like a meal I couldn't digest. Could I summon the energy to renew my search for and make myself part of a new temple? Or was I chasing something that exists only in my memories?

My Geographically Challenged Family

They'd come. They'd go. They'd supercharge my life for a few days, sometimes a week, then go back to theirs. We'd laugh, we'd talk—about things big and small. I'd sleep better knowing they were under my roof. Mornings would bring the warm, familiar company I'd missed. But on the last day of our time together, sadness would rumble beneath the surface, undermining the pure pleasure of their presence. Then: "Bye, Mom. Love you." Off they'd go, until the next time.

As a child I spent part of most days and every birthday, anniversary, and holiday with my dad's parents. Our lives were interwoven with extended family. Special occasions found my parents, sister, and me celebrating with our aunts, uncles, and cousins, and with our beloved grandpa, his warm, quick-to-well-up blue eyes, balding grey hair and mustache above his sweet smile. We'd gather around grandma's damask-covered dining room table, extended with extra boards to make room for everyone except us kids; we sat at card tables covered with tablecloths to look like part of the dining table. Uncle Walt, wiry and wily, quick with a wisecrack; Aunt Jo, the earth mother, plump, with grey curls and a round ruddy-cheeked face; Aunt Ellie, a once-stunning spinster, with fading red hair and pasty white complexion; Uncle Hal, fat and jolly, with sparkling blue eyes. And Aunt Mimsy, Mom's petite, savvy childhood friend with her sweet, balding hubby, Uncle Rob.

In our immediate and extended family, everyone knew and poked their noses into everyone's business. That could be annoying, but there was an upside: caring family who pitched in when help was needed. Too sick to leave the house? Mom's tuna casserole delivered to your door. Parents need a date night? Drop the kids at grandma and grandpa's for a sleepover. Were there sibling squabbles, even rifts in our family? Oh yeah. But when trouble came, disputes melted away like sugar in coffee.

As the ocean-crossing immigrant generation aged, their children were right there to help. A success by any measure. When they retired, would they have left their children, grandchildren, and extended family behind and moved to sunnier climes? Not after the hardships they'd endured to bring siblings across the sea, and to form kinship groups like those they'd been forced to flee.

It was different for my parents' generation, the children of those immigrants. Free from the desperate conditions their parents had experienced, those who enjoyed the means also had the inclination to leave harsh winters behind and head for Sunbelt cities. That generation authored the term 'snowbirds'. They wintered in sunny climes, then returned to the nests they'd made near family and friends.

My generation ignited flames that flared up, then blazed into our mobile society. Unlike our parents, many of us 'went away' to college, the military, or the Peace Corps and often kept going—chasing job opportunities, romantic relationships, and shiny new lifestyles. Our children's college and career choices? Unconstrained by proximity to home.

Now we look around at the detritus left by those flames: families scattered across the country or beyond borders; aging parents stranded.

I'm lucky. My children keep up a steady stream of visits and I'm logging lots of frequent flyer miles going to see them in California, North Carolina, and Arizona. Our times together fill me up. When I drop into their full lives, I appreciate the ingredients that flavor their lifestyles: the people they see, the places they go, the rhythm of their households. Before a visit ends, someone says, "Let's figure out when we'll see each other again." Phone calls, FaceTime and cyber-messages keep us connected. But between those electronic contacts, life happens.

Parting is easier when *I* leave *them*. When they leave me, I relive the heartache I felt when they left the nest. I didn't know I'd experience that pain over and over again.

On a quick visit, it's easy to follow Will Roger's advice: *Never miss a good chance to shut up.* It's easy to keep things light when your time together is brief. If we lived in the same zip code, would we get on each other's nerves? Would grievances fester into rifts? I remember squabbles my parents had with their siblings at family dinners. And what they said when we got home:

"Ellen's such a control freak. I don't know how Frank puts up with her."

"It's awful how they coddle their kids. They should try saying 'no' once in a while."

"Can't Norma cook anything but that jaw-breaking flank steak?"

But if trouble struck, they were there for each other in a heartbeat.

I'd love to hear, "I baked an extra lasagna for you; I'll stop by later to drop it off." Or, "Want me to go to the doctor with you? I know you're freaked out about it."

There are times when those grown-up children would welcome some over-the-top mothering. If we lived near each other, they'd gain an EZ pass to adult-only time, with no meter running, and their children would discover an age-old pact: what happens with grandma stays with grandma.

I travel to celebrate my grandchildren's milestone events, but I'd rather be around when we're just hanging out; and help my daughters with errands or household tasks. Instead, they treat me like a guest:

"Just go to the table, Mom." Then: "Leave your dishes."

What kind of mom lets her daughter wait on her? The kind who isn't around enough to know her way around the kitchen.

"The next best thing to seeing the kids arrive is seeing their headlights dim as they leave," some friends wryly observed. I can't imagine feeling that way. Do their visits turn my quiet life upside down? Yes. Do I love it? Yes. Since time is short, we jam in as much as we can—sightseeing, board games, browsing through photo albums. I'm never ready for our time together to end. When the moment comes, I wave goodbye, smiling through a blur of tears.

Get a life, I've told myself. Let them get on with theirs. But I wish the pendulum would swing back: there's a reason we call our loved ones *nearest* and dearest. Drop-in visits beat those by reservation. When it comes to family, getting and giving hugs should not require advance planning.

The Presence of Absence

Absence: A state or condition in which something expected, wanted, or looked for is not present or does not exist.

Merriam Webster

It's the quiet.

Vaguely present in the first weeks after Dan died.

Then a distinct, impossible to ignore, unsettling daily companion.

Quiet, once so welcome, with two infants a year apart.

At midlife, after work, coming home to clamoring children's voices:

"Can we eat soon? I'll be late for practice!"

"Will you help with my book report?"

"I lost my permission slip! The field trip's tomorrow!"

Back then I savored the quiet that followed "G'night, sweet dreams."

Later, in career-capping years, after a multi-tasking, no-time-to-pee day at a cacophonous, chaotic workplace, followed by the chatter and clatter of the crowded commuter train, I appreciated my man-of-few-words spouse. On weekends, in search of silence, I'd take walks in the woods or drives in the country.

When my career was in full swing, and later, when launching a consulting practice from my home office, Dan and I regrouped at dinner.

"This rotisserie chicken's good," I'd say. "Where's it from?"

"Costco. I like it too."

"Figure out the web hosting thing?"

"I'm down to two choices."

"Jenna called. She might have a meeting here next month."

"Great! Hope she stays a few days."

It was easy to work from home with a husband used to spending his days alone, an introvert by nature. I, too, enjoyed the quiet.

Then suddenly, when he died, I discovered a different kind of quiet:

No "Good morning."

No "It seems cold in here. Should we turn up the heat?"

No "We're out of milk. What else do we need from the store?"

No sounds of someone in the house, puttering around the kitchen, shutting a door, rustling the newspaper. Just the ring of the phone, the ping of the microwave, the bark of the dog, and scary nocturnal house sounds broke the silence.

In 1624, when John Donne wrote the meditation "No Man Is an Island," he'd just lost his beloved wife, and London was in the throes of the Great Plague, a mysterious disease with no known cause or cure. No wonder his words echo through the centuries, stating what I was experiencing firsthand: human beings fare badly when isolated from others; we need to be part of a community to thrive.

Until Dan died, I hadn't realized that marriage had shielded me from silence—even in our dotage, when most conversations were quick exchanges:

"When's your next dental appointment?"

"My car's due for service. Will you take it in?"

Now I see that those modest placeholders—keeping the lines open for important exchanges—stood between me and solitude. My husband and I were a tiny community unto ourselves. In his absence, quiet descended.

Quiet—once a luxury, a welcome break from a house full of children chattering, or an office humming with activity—quiet became a force to contend with, an absence, a void. A constant reminder of the solitude that arrived with and persisted after "death did us part."

The need to escape the silence of solitude pushed me out of the house and into socially fertile situations, forcing me to forge the friendships and other outside interests I hadn't had time to develop while immersed in work. After many misses but some hits—a multi-year volunteer project and a friendly bridge game—my calendar and my life filled with the welcome sounds of convivial conversation and light-hearted laughter. It took years of effort.

From time to time, when the kids and grandkids visited, or a plane ride would bring me to them, sounds of life returned—kids giggling, hair dryers whirring, showers running. Too soon, bags would be packed, my chest would tighten. After goodbye hugs and kisses, the silence in my home seemed louder.

> *Resources for new widows tend to ignore how keenly the everyday presence of a spouse is missed. New widows miss the everyday chitchat that keeps the lines of communication open and the comfort of their husband's physical presence. Painful awareness of these 'absences' will recede in time.*

Phase Three

Searching for A Few Good Friends

While married, raising children, engaged with friends and colleagues, 'alone' time was a luxury. But as a new widow, relieving solitude became my number-one goal.

Although it was a hard slog to show up over and over again to rooms filled with strangers, in time I found some kindred spirits who became good friends. But all of them were women. From my teens through my years in the workplace and in social situations, I'd always enjoyed the company of men. As a widow, my existence was eerily devoid of them. Finding male friends? A hard nut to crack.

Lonely? You're Not Alone

I define connection as the energy that exists between people when they feel seen, heard, and valued; can give and receive without judgment; and derive sustenance and strength from the relationship.

Brené Brown, Ph.D.

One day I received a survey from my temple for "households with only one adult member." They'd found that twenty-five percent of members fit that description. How, they wanted to know, could they better serve them?

I wondered, who are those single members? Once married; divorced; widowed like me; never married, not yet or not interested—had I forgotten anyone? I completed the survey, but I wondered why it hadn't asked the jackpot questions: Are you lonely? How can we help?

Gerontologist Dr. Bill Thomas calls loneliness, boredom, and helplessness the "three plagues." I'd suffered from all three: loneliness often breeds boredom; when I couldn't fill that void, I'd feel helpless. In this big, wide, wonderful world, isn't boredom some kind of personal sin? Felt like it.

⁂

Several years into widowhood, my circle of friends had grown; so now someone would usually ask, "How about a movie this weekend?" Or, "Want to meet at the farmer's market Saturday?" Weekdays would offer up social and substantive fare—planned and impromptu. But sometimes, Friday would roll around with nothing but white space on my weekend calendar.

"Get busy," I'd tell myself, "find something to do." But I couldn't always muster enough energy and ingenuity to carpe the diem. Can you keep a secret? I'd binge-watch TV, milking my streaming subscriptions for all they're worth. Sometimes, on the weekend, I'd go to the grocery store or to Starbucks just to interact with other human beings. No substitute for engaging with friends or family—but it sure beat sitting home with my dog all weekend.

When I was married, mothering, and immersed in my career, a drive in the country offered soul-reviving solitude. Since I've lived alone, not so much.

During those weekend stints in solitary confinement, when my children would call from their dots on the map and ask how I was doing, I'd never answer, "isolated, longing for company." We'd catch up, schmooze, and plan our next visit.

※

Meetup CEO Scott Heiferman says that America faces a "loneliness epidemic." Research confirms that social isolation is increasing. Why? Because today's way of life reduces the quantity and quality of our relationships. Fewer people live near family. Many delay getting married and having children. More people of all ages are living alone.

Since losing Dan, like the old song says, I was "alone again, naturally." I spent years walking into rooms of name-tagged strangers—joining, volunteering, looking for social connections. At the January meeting of a discussion group, when we'd shared New Year's resolutions, I'd said, "To find a new best friend."

I'd left my BFF behind—tearfully—when we'd left Houston. That friendship, steeped in shared confidences from our children's playdates through their wedding days, seemed irreplaceable. Although she's a phone call away, as a widow I'd needed someone nearby who cared about me and to care about, someone to count on for companionship and support.

Turned out that desire was not just wishful thinking, but essential to my health. The trend that prompted my congregation's survey, concerns medical professionals as well. Dying of loneliness isn't just an expression. Social psychologist

Bert Uchino found that people with little social support have a mortality rate as high as alcoholics; conversely, the impact of making friends has a comparable effect on your health as giving up smoking. A primitive, primal need for connection is hardwired into our brains. No wonder I'd felt an urgency to fill that void.

Harvard's eighty-five-year study on adult happiness concluded: "Good relationships keep us happier and healthier. Period." Having someone to rely on helps your nervous system relax, keeps your brain healthier for longer, and diminishes both emotional and physical pain. Study director Dr. Robert Waldinger noted, "It's the quality of your close relationships that matters." I didn't need a research study to reach the same conclusion.

My congregation reflects a societal trend. Psychologist Susan Pinker's research revealed that people "with frequent face-to-face interactions were not only physically and emotionally healthier, but also lived longer…" Sadly, Pinker notes, "a quarter of the population says they have no one to talk to."

The most popular category among Meetups' fifteen million U.S. members? Socializing. In transient Washington D.C., an especially challenging place, even for someone with an outgoing personality like mine, to find and develop an emotionally intimate friendship.

Aristotle said, "Friendship is a slow-ripening fruit." Although I'd urgently needed a new best friend, the process required time; first to find a kindred spirit, then to deepen the connection. Time to share our stories, to color and fill in the background; so when we ask, "what's new?" the answer would fit into a full, nuanced narrative. It required honesty, the willingness to give and receive confidences in the quest for understanding. Impatience aside, it was worth the wait.

A confidante is a woman "with whom private matters and problems are discussed." When I called a friend recently—someone I've become close to over several years—I explained why I hadn't called recently:

"I've been an emotional wreck, worrying about Stacy's health. I was waiting for an update before I called." She listened. We talked.

As we hung up she gently chided, "You didn't have to wait. You could've picked up the phone to tell me, 'I'm in a funk'." Our friendship, she was telling me, could handle the raw, unprocessed stuff of life. Mission accomplished.

Kissing a Lot of Frogs...

Wanted: The company of a warm, open-hearted, intelligent, fun man.
Must love children, dogs, movies, new experiences and not weigh less than me.

While searching for women friends, I realized that I also missed the company of men. Dan was gone, and I'd left behind the men I'd befriended at work. I didn't want a romantic relationship, but I wanted—no *needed*—the company of a male friend.

One morning an article in the New York Times self-care section caught my eye: *Finding Female Friends Over Fifty Can Be Hard. These Women Figured It Out.* While mentally challenging the notion that 'over fifty' is a significant designation, I bumped up against this quote:

"There were meet-ups for those in their twenties, thirties, and forties, but nothing for older women," said the founder of a group in San Francisco. "And I didn't want men."

Really? No men? Having gold-medaled in "finding friends over sixty-five," when I started my search, I'd set out to find friends of both genders but was hard-pressed to find male friends.

It never occurred to me to look for female friends only. Growing up, I'd sit with the men when my parents had company. In high school I hung out with guys as well as girls—ask me about the batting averages of our home team heroes. I'd enjoyed the workplace because it mirrored life, offering not only mixed company but dynamic interaction with women and men from across the country and the world.

So the article made me wonder: Why would some women exclude men from their circle of friends? Sure, there's a special comfort and candor among women, and some topics I reserve for 'just us chickens', but is that symptomatic of a social-selection process that narrows our closest friendships to those with backgrounds most similar to ours? Do college-educated post-career women like me pretty much stick to our own kind? Are we so weary of life in a male-dominated society, of making our way—or being thwarted, sidelined, or stepped over—in a man's world, that we're painting all men with the same brush? I get why women prefer the camaraderie of women; so do I. But I like to have men in my life.

I understand the impetus that inspired the woman who started the age-specific MeetUp group. No doubt the MeetUp group includes women from diverse backgrounds with many points of view. But life without men? Boring! Friendships limited to one's own gender and age group? Too artificial and sterile for me.

So, five years into widowhood, I dipped my toe in the water of online dating. The profile questionnaire didn't allow me to post my 'Wanted' message, but I plunged in anyway.

My first date, a once-prominent journalist, was like an old newspaper clipping—stuck in the past, faded, and stale. At dinner, the words 'captive audience' took on new meaning for me as he nursed his cup of soup for twenty minutes, then gave each morsel of food loving attention, but gave me none, not asking a single question or making any attempt at conversation.

The next day he called. I let voicemail answer. For weeks Mr. Groundhog Day called again and again, creepily introducing himself and leaving the exact same message each time. So my foray into online dating began in a sadly disturbing way.

My next date, an upbeat, easygoing guy, had chosen a funky, intriguing lunch spot. We'd shared an interest in architecture, so I'd welcomed his spontaneous, "C'mon, I'll show you some Victorian homes nearby." But before my seat belt had clicked he'd secured a place on my 'never again' list. His car had smelled like my husband's: a noxious blend of man-sweat, fast food, and artificially sweetened air freshener.

Then I found someone who looked like a great match: a War-on-Poverty veteran like me. When I read his profile to a friend she said: "He sounds perfect for you!"

Mr. Seemed-Right and I hit it off. He said he'd like to see me again; fine with me. He was working to engage new generations in Civil Rights. "I'm involved in a similar project," I'd exclaimed, "I'll connect you to my colleagues." Fatal mistake: I'd turned our date into a meeting. The only contact since? Emails copying me on plans to link the projects.

Up next, a retired lawyer who lived on the opposite side of our sprawling county, connected by a toll road. "I don't have an EZ pass," he confessed (really?). So I made the long trek to our coffee date. Mr. Needs a Secretary chose a Starbucks (be still my heart). But when we entered the tiny establishment, *surprise*—the few tables in the tiny shop had been *occupado*. "Let's walk over to the grocery store," he said, "sometimes you have to think outside the box." (And come up with Safeway?) We talked. We didn't laugh. I downed my coffee in record time.

Another wannabe suitor insisted we meet at his home. While showing me in, he paused lovingly at his wife's bridal portrait.

"Uh-oh," I'd wanted to tell him. "You just violated Rule No. 1 of Geezer Dating."

But I realized then that online dating is no way to find a friend. Widowers want a replacement wife, not a buddy. Me? Been there, done that. I was lonely but liberated.

I responded to another prospect who sounded like a down-to-earth guy I might enjoy hanging out with. His emails had been breezy: "Your profile's great. Hate eating alone. How about dinner?"

For our dinner date I wore a sweater and scarf with simple earrings. He wore a grey zip-up fleece jacket, chinos, and tennis shoes that matched his washed-out complexion. The conversation and his life? Equally dull. Mr. Blah: "So, you worked with non-profits. I've got a non-profit client, the West Point Class of '52. They don't do much." (*Neither did he; his 'boutique CPA practice' kept him busy one month a year.*)

"Let's try the pasta bar," he'd said, "It'll be fun. And we get ice cream."

I knew this paunchy guy would pile his plate high. (*My way-too-heavy husband had <u>loved</u> buffets.*) The buffet offered linguini, penne, or fusilli. He'd asked, "What's the funny-looking kind again? Give me that with six meatballs and extra cheese."

He'd golfed that day. "Ooh," he'd moaned, "my legs are killing me." (I wanted to tell him "I'm your date, not your wife"). An audible burp with no "excuse me," rocketed him into the top tier of my worst-dates list. As he nursed his coffee, the dining room emptied. The wait staff and I had the same question: "Are we done yet?"

I concluded that this lonely guy—and others of his vintage—were not only seeking relief from their solitary confinement, but also missed the Mrs., the kind of wife who'd kept their pantry stocked, social calendar full and, they appreciated now, loneliness at bay. But to fill the void required dating, and for that they needed training. I'm developing a syllabus. *Chapter One: She's Your Date, Not Your Wife.*

As for me, lesson learned. Don't look for friends on Match.com

In time I found and enjoyed male company during a weekly bridge game. Did it satisfy my need for male friendship? No. But I couldn't figure out what else to try, so I settled for that.

Staying Single? Suits Me!

Aware of my online dating fiascos, a friend said, "Don't give up. I hope you'll find a keeper."

I knew she meant someone I'd welcome into my life, but my mind flew to the keepers who work at zoos. The dictionary defines 'keeper' as an "attendant, or guard. One that has the charge or care of something." I didn't like the ring of that.

Consider the term 'kept woman', generally reserved for the Other Woman—you know, the one without stretch marks who presumably enjoyed a long-term salacious relationship with a married man who paid the rent for fringe benefits. Was that so different from marriages like mine in which the man 'brought home the bacon' and the woman was lover, companion, and live-in help?

During my seventeen-year child-raising time-out from employment, we'd lived on Dan's salary. He'd earned it, so he felt free to spend it. "Look," my daughter shouted, "Daddy's driving a new red convertible!" He'd splurged on a set of wheels unfit for carpooling, then another time on a fishing boat. But if I had my eye on a pricey pendant, I wouldn't buy it for myself. Instead, I'd hint and hope. Would he buy it for me? Had I been a good little wife?

※

True, I'd tried online dating, but I was looking for male companionship, not marriage. I'm not the only woman of my vintage who doesn't want to hear wedding bells again. Would I welcome a close relationship with a man? Yes! That's why I'd tried online dating. But would I want to share my space 24/7? No! An old song says, "Love and marriage, they go together like a horse and carriage." Well Tra La La, who do you think rides in the carriage, and who pulls it? The lyrics insist: "You can't have one without the other." (I told you it was an old song.)

My mother was 'the perfect woman' for two lucky men. Their needs always came before hers, because they'd worked hard all day (*like she hadn't!*). After fifty years of married life—happily married, then widowed twice—when she tried on her new single status, it felt good: not binding, plenty of room to grow.

No more making, then quickly scuttling her own plans:

"The girls are going to a movie."

"Oh? You told Bob we'd play bridge? I'll say I'm busy."

Or, "Sure, we can skip the party. I'll make dinner."

Luxuriating in her late-life freedom, she took up oil painting and sang in a choir. She and her friends bought season tickets for the symphony and ballet.

Before, when our family visited, she'd spent every possible moment with us. Not anymore.

"We're going to the beach, want to come?"

"You go ahead, dear. I'm going to take a bath."

Now I'm on my own after a forty-year marriage. I miss my husband but understand how Mom felt. Yes, as I've said, I'd like a man in my life for fun, companionship, and affection, if one were to come along. But share my space on a full-time basis? When the clock strikes bedtime, I want to be home. Alone. Eat what I want to, when I feel like it. Meals? Like Saturday Night Live skits: I use whatever's available and have it fork-ready in five minutes. The clock would start when I scoped out the fridge, freezer, and pantry and end when I sat down to eat. Do I want to confer with my male buddy about what to eat for breakfast, lunch, and dinner? In the time that it would take, I could've fixed and scarfed down whatever meal we were discussing.

I hated having a roommate in college but happily traded privacy and my own space for the loving comfort of marriage. That was fine until the kids left home. After that, our lives were on different tracks. He was retired, happy to be at home; I held a demanding, exhilarating job that included frequent travel. I could relate to the late comedian Rodney

Dangerfield's comment, "We sleep in separate rooms, have dinner apart, take separate vacations—we're doing everything we can to keep our marriage together."

On a real estate blog, *Living Apart Together: Separate Spaces Keep Couples Close*, one happy couple posted: "Our living arrangement gives us the best of both worlds: togetherness when we want it, alone time when we don't." The author predicted that a growing sense of independence within relationships could lead more modern couples to "live apart together." In fact, it seems that solo oldies lucky enough to find a loving partner are inventing new variations on the togetherness theme. Rather than merging households, some couples maintain their own homes; others take separate apartments in the same building. Builders are offering condos with two master suites. In online dating profiles, for "relationship preferences" I'd check, "Friend, activity partner, companion." I did not check "marriage" because I didn't want—or need—a keeper.

Some widows may wish to have "a man in her life" or choose to have the pleasure of male company on occasion. Whether, when, or to what extent that is desired is a personal preference that will emerge with the tincture of time.

Searching for Community

After exchanging email addresses and good wishes with my bereavement group, I went home and took stock of my situation: no job, no family in town; and Kay, my one good friend. My life was nowhere near as full or intellectually fertile as I needed it to be. Finding community? Daunting, but desperately needed. I think the *Stanford Social Innovation Review* nailed it in this 2015 review of the literature:

> *Members of a community have a sense of trust, belonging, safety, and caring for each other... That treasured feeling of community comes from shared experiences and a sense of—not necessarily the actual experience of—shared history... This feeling is fundamental to human existence.*

I'd hoped to find community when I joined a congregation. Since giving up on that, I'd been floundering. Hmm... where could I find and engage with people with whom I felt at home, socially aware people with similar backgrounds and values?

In my career-capping job I'd helped the founder of a national nonprofit, the Women's Connection, gain financial support to launch this effort: "To create an inclusive community of professional women, fifty and forward, whose changing life situations lead them to seek new connections and opportunities." To evaluate the organization, I'd attended a meeting of the D.C. chapter, so I knew that each month's program included small-group discussions. Now, as a new widow, it seemed like a perfect way for me to discover like-minded women. I couldn't sign up fast enough. Soon afterward I joined the Diversity Committee, convened because the chapter had failed to attract women of color. I saw that Isabelle, the project chair, had a clear plan: this promised to be a successful effort. Slim, poised, clad casually with understated elegance, her close-cropped white hair completed her sophisticated, self-assured presence.

Our committee found partner organizations with a shared purpose: "To learn about women's issues through many lenses—cultural, spiritual, ethnic, historical, and economic." Meeting at coffee shops and diners, we put our networks to good use. We'd brainstorm ideas over lunch at a local diner, then plan joint programs with leaders of African American, Muslim, and Hispanic women's organizations.

I was in my element—working with dynamic, savvy women, meeting with organization leaders, planning programs, writing publicity releases and more. We learned from and about each other, and from the women who attended our programs, so popular we co-sponsored two or three with each partner organization. One day, when I picked up Salem for a meeting, I was surprised to see her without her hijab. Smiling, she'd explained "I only cover in mixed company." After chatting about our children and grandchildren, she mentioned that she represented the Muslim community on a county commission.

On one occasion we met with Nancy Navarro, president of the Montgomery County Council, to discuss her keynote message for our program about immigrant Latina mothers and their American-born daughters. Her face lit up. "Could I stay for the program? I'd love to hear how women are coping with those issues."

Isabelle and I often drove together to scout out venues for our meetings, chatting, as we went from place to place, about our families, careers, and political views. Turned out we had much in common. We became good friends.

When cast out into an ocean of loneliness, your heart lifts when someone throws you a lifeline. That's what Isabelle did for me. We'd talk about anything and everything over long lunches or phone calls. Rooted in the D.C. community, she'd say, "You might like"… and became my guide to organizations that fit my interests and could be fertile ground for friend-finding. One of these, Senior Leadership Montgomery, seemed particularly promising. It was a year-long program for people who'd made their mark in various fields and sought new opportunities. The program also promised behind-the-scenes introductions to our county's governmental and civic organizations. I applied and was accepted. The year-long program met one day a month, but each month's jam-packed schedule left little time to socialize. I didn't make a single friend.

Another suggestion Isabelle made proved more fruitful: a monthly 'lunch-and-learn' program at the Washington Ethical Society. After several months, I'd gravitated to slim, chestnut-haired Laura, a lawyer in her mid-fifties and a native Chicagoan like me. One day she asked, "Would you like to start a book club with me?" Ah. Years later our club is going strong: five women distinctly different from each other—spanning four decades in age. Do we get together socially? Rarely. Unlike me, they have family and friends around. We've come to know each other well and care about each other, but would I invite one of them to go to a movie, or come over for lunch? No, we're not that kind of friends.

At some point I realized that the only time anyone visited me at home was when I hosted the book club. At our next meeting, when the conversation shifted from the book to schmoozing, I mentioned that in Houston, friends and neighbors often dropped by to chat. "Oh," they said in unison. "We don't do that here."

Nestled in a suburban subdivision with sprawling, privacy-promoting front lawns, my neighbors, like chipmunks that dart out to find food, then disappear into their lairs, would venture out to pick up mail or newspapers, then scurry back into their homes. I tried going to homeowners' association meetings, but no joy there. Neighbors visited with each other, not the new kid on the block.

Let's see… what else did I try? Bridge lessons at a senior center—I had to steel myself to go there (age segregation—ugh). No luck there: most of the players were married couples.

After this and other failed attempts, I wanted to give up but knew that would be self-defeating.

For a while I'd get together for lunch with friends from my former job. One of them, single like me, showed up on my calendar every few months. A link to the professional community I missed, she was the only friend dotting otherwise barren weekend landscapes.

Oh, those weekends. When I'd hear, "Have a great weekend," my heart would sink, knowing that Saturday morning I'd wake to a blank calendar and drop into an abyss of solitude. As if responding to a whistle on a frequency widows couldn't hear, from Friday night to Monday morning, the people I'd typically see during the week would vanish.

How to pass the time? I'd walk the dog, go to local stores just to see people and exchange greetings with someone—even a checkout clerk. At home, I'd work on my writing, indulge in a juicy page-turner, and choose from a menu of time fillers (okay, time killers): surfing the web, listening to podcasts, tackling the Sunday crossword—all with a backdrop of silence-breaking TV talk shows. I'd phone an old friend for a catch-up chat; check in with the kids and grandkids. What else? Naps. Online Scrabble with my daughter. And, after checking several streaming services, I'd find a movie, then settle in for the evening. Finally, after what seemed more like a week than a weekend, on Sunday night I'd welcome slumber with a wistful whisper, "another one hits the dust." On dreaded three-day weekends? I'd get out of Dodge—even just for a scenic drive.

Going from solitary confinement to a caring community is a hard slog. But I had to keep trying to reach this elusive goal, because, as the Stanford Review article asserts, it's vital to my well-being.

Phase Four

Coming Into My Own

Looking Back, Moving Forward

In the first years after losing my husband and my career, unsettling emotions sat just beneath the surface, poised to pierce through my defenses or derail my progress. Without warning, I'd descend into an emotional morass of anger, fear, and sadness. But I had to move forward. I began to accept and take charge of matters that had always fallen to my husband: home maintenance, lawn and garden upkeep, and—ugh—tax returns. All of these and more now fell to me. Like holding my nose and getting through required college courses I'd never have elected to study, I gritted my teeth and got up to speed on managing both 'his' and 'her' responsibilities.

Struggling to cope with the sudden shifts in my life, I couldn't begin to imagine myself with renewed enthusiasm for life. Meeting each new day with dull despair, I couldn't see a way that my circumstances could change.

I read about people moving through the stages of grief. I understood that I could and would move through this funk. But I couldn't imagine how. Slowly, with the help of counseling, my support group, my family's loving concern, and my own indefatigable spirit, I did carry on. Those deep disappointments that had taken up residence in my psyche eventually took a backseat to the forward thrust of my life.

Who, Me? Change the Filter, Drain the Pipes?

You hear a scratching noise in the wall. Your dog's ears perk up; he hears it too. You know it must be a mouse.

In a flash you're back in the first weeks as a widow, when the furnace broke down in mid-winter, and the repairman asked, "Is this the original unit?" And you'd answered, "Probably," with no hint of your usual confidence, seconds before he'd answered his own question:

"Oh, we put it in four years ago. Our label's right there."

You'd explained, knowing this old-timer would understand, "My husband took care of the house. I'm new to all this."

But your heart sank. You wondered what else you didn't know that could suddenly become critical information?

In professional roles, when people turned to me in a crisis, over and over again I'd pulled a rabbit out of a hat. I wasn't trained to manage staff, but I'd grown into it. But when it came to the inner workings of a house, I was clueless. And—I realized now—I'd chosen to stay that way. Even now, years after going it alone. After all, when I was growing up, little girls didn't need to bother their little heads about how houses worked. They just had to know how to do housework. A bright child, I'd wanted to be like Daddy someday, out in the world, but I'd known I'd be a wife and mother like Mom, at home taking care of our family.

Mom wouldn't have known about her heating unit either. Just as she'd relied on Dad for all things house and car related, I'd relied on my spouse. Not to do the work, although both Dad and Dan would sometimes take a stab at it, but to deal with the men they paid to do it.

Suddenly, as a new widow, ready or not, house-related tasks fell to me.

I'd learned a lot since being thrust into the homeowner-in-chief role. I'd replaced the filter for my furnace like a champ, and thought I'd gotten the hang of being mistress of the house, until I heard that scratching noise. Suddenly I was six years old, wanting my daddy. Or his adult replacement, my husband. Wasn't that the way it was supposed to work? How could Dan have left me so suddenly, so ill-prepared for this grisly task? Why, I asked for the umpteenth time, still asking even though he was gone—why didn't he take care of himself—couldn't he see that he wasn't the only one affected by his stubborn refusal to see a doctor, to get counseling?

But here I was. It was up to me to deal with this. Was I queasy? Uneasy? No matter. I'd long since accepted that everything formerly on Dan's 'to-do' list now fell to me. But that didn't mean I had to handle his former tasks as he had. So I searched my neighborhood listserv, found a highly rated pest-control service, got out my iPhone, and called. It never occurred to me to tackle the problem myself. Not for one second. I conjured up the cartoon image of a lady on a chair, shrieking, and shaking a broom at a mouse scurrying around below. No way would I engage in mortal combat with the intruder. Gripped by fear, I didn't care if the fear was irrational. Like a child burying her face in Mom's lap at the sight of flying monkeys in the Wizard of Oz, I couldn't risk looking.

The pest control technician set traps in various places. I asked, "Do you come back to dispose of what you catch?" I heard what I feared he'd say, "No, we'd charge for a service call each time. Could you check the traps?"

"Oh, I couldn't," I told him, quite sure that was beyond me.

I called my daughter, a thousand miles away.

"Mom," she says gently, "You'll have to do this yourself."

I shuddered but saw her point. There were nine traps. No telling if or when one of them might spring.

"Turn a plastic bag inside out," she advised. Put your hand in it. Grab the trap and its contents, then reverse the process. You won't have to touch it." My heart sank. I cringed at the prospect of even checking the traps. But what choice did I have?

The next morning, I peeked at one trap, then another. Empty. Whew! But the next was *occupado*. I steeled myself and got the job done. On to the next. Another victim! It was getting easier. Several days later, despite a daily trap-checking ordeal, the score stood at two. At $100 a mouse, it was an expensive lesson, but I knew that this was the first, not the last task I'd have to tackle, because there was no man of the house anymore. My first impulse was no longer "ask not what you can do for yourself, ask who you can pay to do it for you." I'd discovered that, when push comes to shove, I could rely on myself. I won't shriek. I'll roar!

Long after losing my husband, I'd become used to 'flying solo' through life. But every now and then something would remind me that I was going it alone. I'd open my mailbox to find a letter addressed to 'Mr. and Mrs.' And I'd get 'his and hers' ID cards from the insurance company. Annoying but not disturbing.

Making it official still gave me pause. With a lump in my throat, I changed my will to remove my husband as a beneficiary. And when I refinanced the mortgage on 'our' home, I felt the palpable absence of the man who'd bought the house with me—and shared the experience that made it our home. On page after page the line for co-borrower was glaringly blank. Jaws clenched, I removed my husband's name from the deed.

The significance of changing ownership from 'joint' to 'sole' was not lost on me. Although by then I'd been taking changes in stride, this made my emotions well up and spill over.

I thought I'd become used to taking care of business without a second opinion or the benefit of my husband's expertise and experience. No, I didn't know everything he'd known about how the house and car work, or what to do when there's a problem. And sometimes I'd wish I could ask him where to find a tool or how to change a setting. But I'd learned to manage alone, found competent service providers, always sought second opinions, and asked friends and family for advice before making major expenditures.

I'm grateful for Google, because I still have a million questions. I've even begun learning my way around Home Depot. I may not know the lingo, but I've managed to get the help I need from the nice people who work there.

And it no longer surprises me when "change filter on furnace" pops up on my calendar.

Shedding the last documents that testified to my marital status? Painful. But it didn't hurt nearly as much as not being able to delight in and worry about our children's lives with Dan… and watch our grandchildren grow up together. The documents were one-time reminders. Missing the ups, downs, and milestone events of our children and grandchildren? Those reminders go on and on.

A Creative Path to Kindred Spirits

As I entered the Writer's Center annex, my skin felt clammy—was it nerves, the warm summer day, or both? Did I belong there?

Although writing—proposals, promotional materials and such—had been a professional strength, I hadn't dipped my pen into creative writing since high school, and I hadn't felt drawn to it then. But an invitation to write essays for an anthology, and to the sequel, had offered me a way to process the life-altering events of widowhood and retirement that had left gaping holes in my life I was still struggling to fill: close friends and a purposeful intellectual pursuit.

When all of the essays I submitted were included in the published books, I decided to take a writing class at a highly regarded writing center nearby. In the summer course guide, one teacher who drew rave reviews was offering a creative nonfiction workshop. I signed up. Weeks later on a warm summer morning I stepped into a room in the Center's annex, adjacent to the main building. A dozen or so participants, ranging in age from early twenties to middle age, sat on fold-up chairs at narrow portable tables arranged in a square. Wall-hung air conditioning units were locked in a contest with July's heat and humidity.

Sharon, our petite, soft-spoken instructor, casually clad in linen shirt and khaki slacks, introduced herself and asked us to do the same. She explained that our work should be considered first drafts and asked us to offer each other only positive feedback. Then she asked a handsome, thirtyish man to read the material he'd brought. As he began, the exquisite prose I heard made me eye the exit. But as others read their work, I took heart; that first reader was by far the best writer in the group.

Here's how it went: we'd distribute copies of our essay and read our work aloud. Then Sharon would ask, "What did you like about the essay?" We'd receive comments from classmates and from Sharon, and written notes as well. At home I'd use these notes, especially Sharon's, to make revisions and try to improve my work going forward.

After the last class, as I walked to the parking lot with Sharon, she asked, "Would you like to join my memoir group? We meet once a week in my home."

Yes! I drove home pumped up by the invitation.

Just like my first dip into the waters of those summer workshops, the memoir club members welcomed me, but the quality of their work made me feel like an invasive species.

Some of the group had been working with Sharon for years. One woman wrote such exquisite prose, the rest of us were spellbound when she shared new material for a book she planned to publish. Turned out she teaches creative writing at American University. As we were leaving one day, April, a young woman, announced she'd been accepted in a Master of Fine Arts program. Hmm… these were serious writers. What was I doing here?

Each week as I listened to my classmates' work, I felt my confidence drip, drip, dripping away. I reminded myself over and over again that Sharon had invited me; *she* felt I belonged there. So, though I felt I gained more than I gave in this group, I continued. When the Fall session ended, I signed up for the next one, and the next. And I've kept signing up ever since, sharing essays that probe raw memories and help me process new experiences.

Some of my writing colleagues continued, as I did, for years. As we shared essays probing our experiences, we came to know each other well. Preparing for and participating in the memoir group helped me examine the emotional underpinnings of my experiences, especially the struggles, successes and sources of support I'd found as a widow.

Sometimes after sharing an essay with the group, someone would say," Publish it! Encouraged, I started sending my work to online magazines. Some of my pieces were published in *Better After 50,* an online magazine for women, and in *Huffington Post!*

As the list of my published essays grew, writing gave me a professional identity. Oh, how I'd missed that! I'd send a blast email announcing each publication and post each one on a new 'Author' section of my website. The responses—"I can relate" or "Loved this"—boosted my ego and lifted my spirits.

Writing also gave me, as the Beatles sang, "a ticket to ride." The memoir group didn't meet in August. To escape the heat, the few close friends I'd made would head for the beach or cooler climes. I'd always loved to travel, but I'd traveled solo when my husband wasn't up for it. Dining alone and taking in the sights by myself? Nowhere near as enjoyable as traveling with family or friends. But now I could find kindred spirits at out-of-town writing workshops, where I picked up tips to improve my craft *and* explored new places. Since my first out-of-town writing workshop, 'writing in company' has transformed my summers, bringing me to northern Massachusetts, upstate New York, New Hampshire, and other places.

Now, a decade after the Writer's Center workshop, our memoir group anchors my calendar and enriches my life. Some faces have changed over the years, but the group has stayed largely the same and become much more than a writing group. As we've shared stories of our lives, we've come to know each other in a way different from but as intimately as our closest friends. And we're products of the same generation, shaped by the events and mores of our time.

In the safe space of Sharon's living room, we disclose, discuss, and discover meaning from the raw material of our lives. And we've come to care about each other, so we arrive fifteen minutes before each class to catch up on news:

"I'm taking Cindy to New York for her sixteenth birthday."

"My knee surgery went well; glad it's behind me. Missed you guys."

"We're spending the summer in France!"

Do we see each other outside of memoir club meetings? Rarely. Most of my colleagues have lived in the area for years and have family here, as well as longstanding social relationships. And I, no longer a newcomer to the area, have made a few close friends. But as we've shared the raw material of our lives, we've come to care about each other. When we gather in Sharon's living room, we celebrate milestones and share the experiences of advancing age.

After years of searching for community, I've found my clan.

Taking the Wheel, Steering My Course

Looking out at the bleak landscape as a new widow, I had no clue that a few years later I'd become a bona fide member of a group of accomplished writers and enjoy an encore career as an author, with some pieces published to boot! "I'm all in to writing now," I told anyone who'd listen, maybe to hear that myself. What a hoot!

"I think you're happier now than you've ever been," my niece exclaimed on a recent phone call. Me, widowed, retired for several years, the grandmother of teens, setting one place at my dinner table. *The happiest ever? How could that be?* I quickly thought, "No, I was happiest when I was raising my children." Then just as quickly I realized that wasn't true; that was what I'd been programmed to think and say.

Yes, I loved raising three children, but it was hard. No standards of care to trust, no external review noting " outstanding performance" in some areas, "needs improvement" in others. Adorable babies whose cries couldn't tell me whether they were wet, hungry or ill; toddlers whose safety no amount of childproofing could assure; schoolkids who squabbled with each other or came flying in, crying after a fight with friends; endearing humans-in-progress who lived on the edge, leaving homework or lunchboxes at home, or books, baseball mitts, or ballet shoes at school. Beloved little beings who freaked me out when they were ill, injured, or didn't arrive on the school bus because, oops, they'd forgotten to mention that they had band practice after school. I'd struggled to keep straight three different schedules for my children and their classmates, afraid I'd flunk carpool and leave little ones stranded.

Were those hectic times the happiest in my life? That would be a stretch. Were there wild swings between joy so sweet my heart overflowed and fear so intense my knees buckled? Oh yes. Happily, those children grew up to be caring, confident adults. Today I may suffer when they have setbacks, weigh in on decisions they're making but hey—it's their lives. We call and text daily, always planning the next visit—adults with shared memories, our lives intertwined. Now they're watching out for me instead of vice versa.

A big bonus of this time of life: grandchildren. From infancy to adolescence, pure joy for me. Another role that's so different now than it was in my childhood, when my grandparents and other old people I encountered had withdrawn from active life. What fun it is for me to engage with my grandkids, showing up at school plays—camera-clicking, screaming "Encore!", marveling at science fair projects light years beyond mine, connecting online with them to help with writing assignments or chime in on their daily doings.

⁂

As years passed, mourning receded, replaced by warm memories of the private jokes, everyday moments, and life passages I'd shared with my husband, and the rich, joy-replenishing, mutually supportive relationships I enjoy with the children and grandchildren he loved. I'd think of him when the phone rang and I'd hear my eldest granddaughter announce, "Grandma, I got into UCLA! Or my youngest son say, "Mom, we're getting married!" And, a year later, "Sofia took her first steps!"

Do I miss being married? The sad truth is, the switch in our roles—me going full throttle in a challenging career, him at home minding the kids and the house—took a toll on Dan's ego, and on our marriage. Chronologically we were the same age, but Dan had become an old man just when I'd hit my prime. Eager to see the world, I traveled solo in those years, wistfully watching couples our age holding hands, window shopping, out for a stroll, or seeing the sights while I dined early at a table for one.

So did my niece have a point? Maybe. I love making up my life as I go along, doing what I want to do when I want to do it. Now I'm in the driver's seat. I may be late coming to the party, but I do feel liberated. And it does feel great.

My New Backup Team

When I was twenty-five years old, I left my life as an independent woman in Washington D.C. and moved back to Chicago. My friends said, "You left that War-on-Poverty job in D.C.? Thought you loved it—we envied you. You were the only one in our class who wasn't either married or stuck in a secretarial job, or both. What happened?"

"My father died suddenly. Everything changed. I transferred to the regional office in Chicago to be near my mom. Dan had been waiting in the wings for years. It was time. Within months we were married."

Coming of age in the sixties, just as my father had supported my mother and our family, I'd expected my husband to support me and ours. Just like mom, I'd left the world of work when our first baby arrived. And like her, at mid-life I'd channeled my intellectual and project management skills into volunteer work.

I'd married a CPA. We'd discuss our finances; he'd manage them. During our forty-two-year marriage I pursued professional interests before and after a long time-out as an at-home mom. Any income I brought in? Gravy.

Growing up, my father never showed me how to change a tire or fix a leaky faucet. Why would he? That was "man's work." Did he have a clue about what to do when something in the house malfunctioned? No, but it was his problem, not Mom's. I picture him sitting cross-legged on the floor puzzling over a faulty electrical outlet. Eventually he'd call a contractor and chat him up so he could do it himself next time. Dad handled all money matters; he didn't even expect Mom to balance her checkbook. Back then, gas station attendants checked the tires and added air if needed. So I never learned how.

The same was true of housekeeping skills. I was raised as if to the manor born but the *manor* I was born to employed a cleaning lady once a week. Mom followed recipes to prepare simple meals, applied her exquisite taste to beautify our home, and entertained with flair. Waxing floors and ironing? That's why she had help. So Mom taught me how to entertain guests, not how to keep house. I learned to cross my legs at the ankle, not how to get windows squeaky clean. I was prepared to be the lady of the house, not a housewife. But I'd married a man, not royalty; we lived in a city apartment, then a house, not a landed estate.

Dan managed home and car repairs. Like my Dad, he chatted up repairmen and mechanics, sounding like he understood what they were saying. He'd translate for me: "The fan belt was loose." Oh. Oil changes and such? On his to-do list, not mine. Same with the gardener; hubby huddled with him; somehow the grass stayed green, and leaves left the premises. I imagine that most married couples divvy up the tasks of running a household. When a husband or wife dies, suddenly their widow or widower has no 'helpmate'.

❧

I've always been happiest nurturing relationships and ideas. I'd never wanted or needed home management skills, but as a new widow I acquired a daunting portfolio of new jobs. Even tax prep and finances. For math-phobic me? I pictured Dan's annual tax-time ritual, covering the breakfast table with IRS forms, green ledger papers, and year-end statements, and tapping away at his adding machine, long after computers could've made the job easier and the data available to me and to another CPA. My role in all this? "I need your W-2s and charitable donations." On money matters, Dan got into the weeds, weighing investment options with our financial adviser. I chimed in at decision times.

You might expect that I'd have panicked, worried that I'd have to carry on alone with all the money and a myriad of other matters outside my comfort zone. But I was incredibly lucky: like a Motown singer, I had back-up. I knew I could count on my three super-kids, all grown up, ready and able to help. With anything. And everything.

Sandra—with those blue eyes and long, almost-white hair—is happiest alone, enjoying her garden or heavily wooded surroundings. The single mom of two teenage girls, she learned the ins and outs of maintaining a large home because, when married, her neurosurgeon husband was always at work, on-call or traveling.

"Walk around the exterior of the house now and then," she told me. "No one else is checking for potential problems." Thoughtful and caring, she sends snail-mail notes in her big, loopy handwriting with a North Carolina return address: "Hey Mom—thinking of you. Hope you're doing well. Thanks for your love and support."

A planner, she prods me about coming events long before they're on my radar:

"Why do you keep asking if I've found a dress for cousin Joan's wedding? There's plenty of time."

"Because I know you'll wait till the last minute."

Jenna, a researcher by profession, happily digs into the minutia of every matter with me. From her home near Phoenix, she'll text: "Here's an article listing the best products for cleaning wood floors. Happy to discuss." Unlike me, Jenna delights in the details. But like me, she embellishes every story. To update me about my teenage grandson, she might start here: "In fourth grade, his teachers noticed…" Eventually I find out what's up.

Jake solves problems quickly, deftly. He moved to L.A. in his early twenties to pursue a film-making career. On his own since then, he's used his wits and grit to handle day-to-day matters and life choices. Knowing financial decisions stress me out, Jake stepped up. "Let's meet with your advisor during my visit." So that's how we roll: Jake goes to meetings with me or joins our calls. Choosing a cell phone plan, or considering a major purchase? Jake's my go-to-guy.

How incredibly fortunate for me to have three adult children happy to help a mom they know would rather be writing, musing, or schmoozing—not dealing with mundane matters.

Sandra, Jenna, and Jake grew up knowing my priorities: ensuring their well-being and achieving social change. I was the mom immersed in writing a speech, planning an event, or developing a new program. When Dan died, they knew well who I am, both my strengths and my weaknesses—like getting in the weeds for every decision or letting emotion cloud reason—so just as I've always supported and advocated for them, they stepped up to help me navigate the new terrain of household and financial management. And so much more.

Flooded basement? Practical Sandra called: "Don't replace the wall-to-wall carpet. Get carpet tiles with rubber backing. If it floods again, you'll only have to replace the wet ones."

One day the refrigerator stopped working. I called detail-oriented Jenna.

"Send me the dimensions of the space."

She called back: "The brand you had is the only one that fits. I'm texting a link to the store near you with the best price. Order now, they'll deliver tomorrow."

Jenna loves to compare hotel and airline options to find the best deals. I don't. When I'm planning a trip, I call her.

"Do you need travel assistance?" she asks in her best reservations agent voice. We search travel websites and confer. After I've booked my itinerary she says, "We always appreciate your choosing us and look forward to serving you again."

Jake's been my travel buddy since his preteens. He'll ask, "How about Maine next summer?"

Yes. Always yes. When I RSVP'd "yes" for a party in Memphis honoring Jake and his fiancé Anna. Jake called: "We're sharing a house with Anna's sister and her husband. There's a third bedroom, want to join us?"

Hmm, they want to hang out with this old lady?

There isn't a week that goes by when I don't need and promptly receive support from my backup team. Most days I hear from two of them; often all three, just to touch base, but there if I need help. And every day I'm grateful to have their loving attention. I imagine widows without that kind of support could form similar teams from among the people close to them. One of the widows I met in my grief group cobbled together a caring cadre from members of her church choir and garden club. In a pinch, neighborhood listservs can be lifesavers. That's how my friend Anne found help when her basement flooded.

Backed by caring offspring, here's how I navigate situations I find daunting: One wintry day I stopped at the gas station to have the air pressure in my tires checked. I remembered Dan saying that in cold weather it was important to keep the tires inflated. The attendant informed me, "Your front tires are shot." Uh-oh.

I texted Jenna the news, then Jake called; when I filled him in, he asked what size I need. "This will be the easiest thing ever, Mom."

Jenna popped in, "Glad to help research this."

I texted, "Your baby brother's got this." She sent back a thumbs up.

Later I emailed Jake: "I'm going to buy the tires tomorrow."

"Glad you told me," he texted. He sent screen shots of top-rated tires with this note: "Don't pay more than $100 each."

The next day I texted: "Got the *Quatrac*s. $70 each."

"Good job!"

That evening I told a friend, "I bought new tires, today. It was easy." She could hear the pride in my voice.

"With all your accomplishments, I'm surprised that was a big deal for you!"

I realized she'd never been married; unlike me, she's always relied on herself for everything. For me, that small thing *was* a big deal.

Today, I'm the sole owner and occupant of the four-bedroom tri-level house I shared with my husband. It didn't come with a manual. Homeowners know the problems keep coming. Maintaining a home and managing my finances was like being thrown onto the front lines of battle without basic training. But I'm not going it alone.

I may appear to be self-reliant, but look again. Also present are three capable adult children-on-call. I navigate life's waters with confidence, thanks to an ever-ready, loving back-up team.

I Can Do That Myself!

As children develop, they proudly declare the independence that accompanies their newly acquired skills—to use a spoon, drink from a cup, and in time, tie their own shoes. Just try to give them a hand and you'll find out fast that help is *not* wanted. As a widow, years went by before I could, and did, master new skills. For so long, like a toddler turning to grownups for help, I'd deferred to professionals or Dan to help manage our house, cars, and finances. But at a certain point I noticed: something in me had shifted. Instead of dreading the next unexpected problem, like a new teen driver, I was ready to take the wheel, not just to keep my life on an even keel, but to move beyond my comfort zone into domains long relegated to my husband.

Yard care, for instance: I'd listened with one ear when Dan told me, "I hired Tony to take care of the lawn, our neighbor Bill Simons recommended him." My only takeaway was to register the man's name. I'd wave hello to Tony and his crew if I happened to be home when they did their thing.

Now the sole homeowner, I was grateful to have Tony, a friendly guy who showed up with his crew every week. It never occurred to me to ask for anything other than their standard services. Each month he'd give me a handwritten bill torn from a drugstore-variety receipt book with carbon copies, and each December he'd hand me a contract for the next year, which I'd promptly sign.

But several years after Dan died, when I was ready to assume the role of Home Manager, I decided to look for someone who used an environmentally friendly approach to lawn care and had a more businesslike operation.

"I can do this differently," I realized, and felt a surge of energy as I took charge of this and other matters. I interviewed and received estimates from a few companies my neighbors recommended and chose one with expertise in landscaping as well as lawn care. And I ditched the company we'd used for homeowners, personal property, and auto insurance. Weary of dealing with that name-brand, impersonal mega-company, I asked my financial manager for a recommendation and discovered a company that's the polar opposite. Lily, my agent, held a senior position at the firm. After an initial information-gathering process, she tailored each policy to my needs. Several months later, when I called to report that a driver had run a red light and hit my car, Lily answered the phone and asked, "Are you all right? Tell me what happened." A sea change from the "Press 1 for homeowner's, Press 2 for auto, Press 3 for…" well, you know.

I also began to put my own stamp on home maintenance. Instead of Dan's 'if it ain't broke' approach, I decided to install energy-saving double-paned windows. And, weary of dealing with a flood-prone basement, I hired a landscape engineer who addressed the underlying problem, putting an end to the occasional, upsetting disaster scenes and their soggy aftermath. It felt great to get a handle on those household management matters.

And they kept coming: A month later, I woke up to an alarm shrieking from the basement.

One look and I saw it was the alarm for the back-up sump pump. "Oh," I thought, "I'll just push the reset button."

The alarm had other ideas. Ignoring the reset, it blasted away at a sound-barrier-challenging decibel level. I checked the breakers. Everything okay. Hmm. A call to my plumber led to a quick diagnosis.

"That battery must be dead. I put it in a long time ago. I'll install a new one."

The house must've loved seeing my shoulders drop, my spirits lift, knowing this was far from over.

Hours later, soon after the plumber arrived with the new battery, he emerged from the basement with this news: "We have a world of trouble." He sat down a safe distance from me to discuss the situation.

"When I pulled out the main pump and the back-up, I found that tree roots had invaded the back-up pump. You'll have to replace both pumps. I'll order them. Meanwhile, if it looks like rain, call me. I'll bring over a small pump I have and hook it up to a garden hose."

Moments later, dollar signs flashing in my mind, I watched him drive away. And watched him drive up again a few days later to install the new units.

"It'll just take me an hour or so," he said.

Three hours later he told me, "I pulled out the old pumps and got rid of those roots. Then I found that your pit's dimensions can't accommodate the pump I brought. I called around and found one that will fit. I'm going out to get it."

"Okay, but I have to leave at 3 o'clock."

"No worry, I'll use the basement door. Just remember to lock it when you get home."

When I arrived home hours later, after sundown, my heart sank as I turned into my driveway and saw his truck there. Dollar signs flashed in my head again, adding the cost of a full day of the plumber's time on top of the price tags for two pumps and a battery.

That night I told my daughter, "Crisis averted, but my mother always said, 'Bad things come in threes.'"

The house must've been licking its lips in anticipation as I slept peacefully that night. The next morning, rubbing sleep from my eyes, I turned on the faucet in the bathroom sink. Nothing happened. I tried again. Not a drop. Kitchen sink? Same story. Basement sink? No luck.

Called the plumber. Another problem to solve as the house and I aged together.

But as these problems arose, where were the frantic, stomach-clenching reactions? What had happened to the woman overwhelmed by financial and home ownership matters? Replaced by the calm problem-solver I'd always been.

I can't count the times that well-meaning people, including my children, asked, "Wouldn't an apartment be easier, and better for you socially?

Ugh. That held no appeal for me. "I've lived in high-rises," I'd tell them. "People I'd see in the elevator or lobby didn't say much more than 'Hello.' And most apartments won't welcome a fifty-pound sheepdog. Even if they did, why would I want to walk him rain or shine, in daylight and after dark, on hot summer days and wintry nights? Now I just open the door, and he can chase squirrels, bark at deer, and visit with the neighbors' dogs."

Those were the reasons I gave, but between us chickens, here's why an apartment holds no appeal: I like my privacy.

I did go out with a realtor once to look for a smaller home to rent. That came to a screeching halt when I asked, "Does the landlord take care of outside maintenance?"

"No," she said, "in our area, renters are responsible for home maintenance."

Why uproot myself for a new set of headaches? That left only one more arrow in the realtor's quiver: a high-rise apartment. As we walked down a long, dark hallway, passing identical, numbered doors, my throat constricted. The two-bedroom apartment she showed me on the tenth floor had a wall of glass overlooking a concrete jungle. The harsh, cold opposite of the bay windows in my home overlooking lush lawns and heavily wooded lots. Then, seeing my expression when I saw the third of three tiny closets, she said, "Oh, but there's a storage space in the basement as well." That turned out to be a wire cage about four feet across, four feet high and six feet deep. I flashed back to one just like it we'd had in our first apartment, before we'd collected a lifetime of belongings. After that outing with the realtor, I fled back to the clutter, comfort, closets, and capacious cellar of my four-bedroom house. I realized that home maintenance was less important to me than the comfort of staying in a home I love, nestled in nature, with neighbors I'd known for years.

When my daughters were teens, those years when peer pressure colored their choices, I gave them *Free to Be You and Me*, by Marlo Thomas, a book described as "celebrating individuality and challenging stereotypes." Written with a view toward empowering children and adults, that book also gave *me* permission to hang up my apron, pass the torch of volunteer leadership, and pursue a path-setting career.

In my new solo role, when a household problem hit, I'd call Sandra in a panic; she manages her large home. Five years later, I was ready to take charge of both home maintenance and personal matters. If that meant learning to manage the business side of life, I was confident that I could grow into those roles just as I'd done when I'd led a dynamic non-profit with fifty employees at a dozen sites. I hadn't welcomed the business side of that either—there'd been a steep learning curve—but I'd plunged in and learned to review financial statements, prepare tax returns, and negotiate salaries with new hires. *That woman—the former nonprofit CEO—was back.*

Now I began assessing the financial professionals I'd engaged since losing Dan. I kept our investment advisor, Tim, who'd come to know our family, had managed our affairs well, and understood my priorities. I'd review each monthly statement, ask a question now and then, and—with Jake present or calling in—confer with him at decision points. He'd recommended a CPA to do my taxes, something Dan had always done.

"I work with Paul Matthews," Tim said. "I can interface with him about your accounts."

So, I'd been paying Paul's firm a hefty sum to prepare my tax return. But not anymore: This year, like a child who's learned to tie her own shoes, I can proudly say, with the help of TurboTax, "I can do it myself!"

Most married couples have unwritten understandings about who does what when it comes to childcare, household chores, and home maintenance. New widows overwhelmed by responsibilities that were in their husband's domain can seek help. In time they'll learn to "do it themselves."

Phase Five

Ready or Not, Here Comes Change

While finding my way through the often rugged, sometimes tedious terrain of widowhood, life went on for our children, grandchildren, and lifelong friends. Graduations, weddings and the loss of a beloved pet brought up a surge of emotions and heightened awareness that my husband was absent, not sharing these milestones with me.

A Bad Case of Being Stuck

If I were a car, my gas gauge would be flashing 'empty'. Or I'd be hoisted up on a mechanic's lift spinning my wheels. Get the picture? I had a bad case of being stuck in place. I'd try to read but find my mind wandering. I'd sleep late, watch too much TV, eat too much ice cream. The hours would drag by.

There's no point contemplating my navel to discern the cause. Nothing major will be found. Then why the inertia? "Maybe it's the winter blues," a friend suggests. "Or the daily drumbeat of crisis-craving cable news."

But I'd felt this way before; I suspected that something was germinating in my subconscious. Underneath the topsoil layer, some new growth was forming, waiting to push through, to make itself known. Then I'd have something—an insight, an inspiration—that blasts the blues away. At least I hoped that would happen again.

I thrive on change. After years of widowhood, life seemed too comfortable, too predictable for my taste.

After my relocation by choice, retirement by accident, and widowhood by surprise, I'd poured my energy into developing close friendships, intriguing activities, and channels for creative expression. No family or friends with shared memories nearby, no colleagues with common purpose—I'd started at square one to build a new life.

"All that effort paid off, Mom," my daughter observed. "I bet you have more going on in your life than most people." Now years after the sudden loss, the steep learning curve and the long, lingering loneliness my calendar fills, not only with weekly yoga and writing classes or monthly book club and women's 'life support' groups, but with lunches, movies, cultural outings, potluck dinners and civic action huddles. When weekends near with no plans in place, someone in my patchwork quilt of friends' texts, "How about a movie?" or "Bridge Sunday?" Am I grateful for each friendship, each welcoming social or mind-stretching affiliation? Yes. Am I content? Well…not lately.

While circling in my holding pattern, I turned to blogs and podcasts for inspiration. One message came through: happiness is a choice; act happy and—in time—you'll feel happy. Centuries old and current research agree: Smiling elevates your mood. So, while I'm watching for the next new thing to grab my imagination, twirl me around and lift my spirits, I'll give that a try. Who knows, if I smile my way through the doldrums, I might crack open a way to see, grasp, and dive into an exhilarating new calling.

Dan died before I'd launched my consulting practice. In that life-changing moment my identity dissolved. After forty-two years, I wasn't a wife, I was a widow. And after a challenging, deeply satisfying career, I had no job, no professional status, none of the exhilarating challenges that engaged my head and my heart.

I didn't expect to remarry, but I did expect to continue my career. When that didn't happen, I hit an emotional wall. But as time passed, mourning receded, replaced by warm memories of private jokes, everyday moments, and passages I'd shared with my husband, and the rich, joy-replenishing, mutually supportive relationships I enjoy with the children and grandchildren he loved.

My husband's long decline prepared me—to some extent—for losing him. But I was not prepared for the other, profound losses: absorbing, purposeful work for me. That I grieve for still.

Nine years a widow, here's where I was:

- Serving on national boards with men and women from mid- to post-career.
- Playing bridge in mixed company.
- Pursuing an encore career, writing essays and a memoir with colleagues of both genders.

Still, something was missing: a challenging volunteer role. What would play to my strengths? How could I contribute in a substantive way? After considering some options, I'd contacted the workforce development director at a local non-profit to explore possibilities. Thought I'd found a great match. After reviewing my LinkedIn profile, he wrote, "We'd like you to lead a workshop and be a guest panelist during our jobseeker boot camps. Then we'll pair you with one participant to mentor." He never called.

Retired Executive—Will Work for Smiles

I love essay writing, but I still had an itch I can't scratch: putting to use my expertise in leading nonprofit organizations. Once in a while, someone would dip their bucket into my well of experience for advice. I'd welcomed those requests, but they hadn't satisfied that itch, so I'd met with our county's fifty-plus volunteer network director to find a local nonprofit I could help. Days later she'd emailed: "I found a match." That led to an organization serving teens in the juvenile justice system. Seemed like a fit, but the organization was running on fumes. Stretched so thin, they didn't have anyone with time to work with me.

Then Linda called. A social entrepreneur I'd worked with in my former job, Linda had founded an organization to unite siblings separated by the foster care system. After building a national network of summer camps for these siblings, she'd passed the leadership torch. Like me, she'd expected to continue helping the organization once she left, but her successor had never sought her advice, invited her to speak on behalf of the organization, or asked to tap her extensive network.

"I called to share an idea with you. I know other founders in our network were shocked to be ignored or worse—treated callously by their successors. Would you consider writing about this with me? We could interview our colleagues about their transitions and brainstorm solutions with them that could inform the field."

I was intrigued—not just to analyze why founders experience such harsh treatment when they move on, but also because this project connected me again to a community I'd missed.

"That's a great idea. We have stories to tell and colleagues who'd jump at the chance to participate."

We jumped in, putting an idea into action as we'd done before. We invited ten former colleagues, and developed a questionnaire to guide each participant, including each other, through a review of our leadership transitions. We'd created our organizations to address a chronic social problem, established a national following, and cultivated relationships with the movers and shakers in our fields. At midlife and mid-career, all of us had been shut out by our successors. We wanted to explore why.

Two years into the project, the *Philanthropy Journal* article published our article. Oh, it felt good to be contributing to my field again!

Then I thought about my cousin's request for help. And it dawned on me: SCORE's a network of retired business executives. Like me! I dashed off an email: "Does SCORE serve nonprofits?"

The answer came back. "Yes!" I completed the application and clicked 'Send'. Will this lead to purposeful, fulfilling engagements in advancing social change? Or another dead end? Several years into retirement, like a car with a lot of mileage that still gets you where you're going, I'm rarin' to hit the highway. Newer doesn't mean better. And I work for free! Why was this so hard?

Paddling Upstream and Down

"Hi. "I believe you have *Jewish Weddings Now* on hold for me."

"It should be on that shelf," the librarian answered, "alphabetized by last name."

"Thanks, and could you recommend a mystery writer like Harlan Coben? I need a good old-fashioned page-turner."

As I left the library, my body announced, "Emotion overload. Spillage imminent." My mind froze, confused by the simultaneous eruption of joy and terror. I felt like a wave that had crashed onto the shore, exuberant in its release but suspended in time, unable to rejoin nature's ebb and flow.

I needed a book to sink into because, in the midst of incredible happiness and profound gloom, I'd descended into a fog reminiscent of the early onset of grief.

"I can't write. I can't even read," I'd told my daughter. "I tried a John Grisham novel but couldn't get into it. Started an

Elmore Leonard mystery, but no luck. It's not the books, it's me. I've got the attention span of a toddler."

⁂

Jake is engaged! I'm overflowing with joy. He found someone he loves who loves him as much as I do. I'm crazy about her. When they call, laughter tumbles from their voices. They're including me in every step of the wedding plans.

But my dog has cancer. I'd found out yesterday, after waiting a week, waiting all day every day for the biopsy results. He doesn't know he has a tennis-ball size mass encircling his intestine. I was clueless, too, when I'd brought him to the vet to check out a minor skin irritation.

Now I'm gathering that my precious pet, Toto, my sole companion during my initiation into widowhood and the new normal that's evolved in the nine years since—that loving companion who sleeps next to me each night, the bed hog I move to make room for, that warm comforting canine—will be leaving me, alone and adrift again in the abyss of mourning. How can this be happening? Toto, whose dark grey shaggy sheepdog countenance and Mr. Congeniality disposition instantly convert strangers to friends and make workmen drop what they're doing to play with him? Who stands guard to protect me every time I take a shower? Who grew up with my grandchildren? Who tried, but couldn't save my husband's life, racing back and forth from the front door to me, alerting me that Dan had started the car but—because his heart had stopped—hadn't left the driveway? Toto, fifty pounds of love. *I'm going to lose him.*

"The X-ray showed it hasn't spread," the kindly vet told me. "The first step is to see an oncologist to find out what your options are. At eleven, he's not young, but he's not ancient either."

"If he were your dog, what would you do?"

"Well, if I had all the money in the world… Surgery could cost thousands. See what the oncologist says. If you decide to do nothing, he might do fine for a while." *A while? What does that mean?* "If needed, we can give him prednisone. For now, add probiotics to his diet."

Prednisone? I'd heard of it but had no idea what it is. Seemed like I'd be boning up on worrisome terms and topics I've avoided till now.

Hours later Jake called: "Got your email. Sorry, Mom. We all love Toto. When will you see the oncologist?"

Then this evening: "Great news, Mom! We're about to seal the deal with the wedding venue. I just sent you the contract. Would you look it over and call me?"

When I called back, I said, "The contract's based on eighty guests. How many are you inviting?"

"Eighty-six ."

"Don't think eighty will attend."

"No worry, we only pay for the number who do."

"And why two cakes?"

"That's just how they priced it. We want a chocolate cake on top of a lemon cake."

Is this real? I'm delving into wedding plans, hours after hearing Toto's dire diagnosis?

"Amanda's excited about having a Jewish wedding. She grew up with no religion."

"That's so great! She's the best. I love how warm and genuine she is." The conversation shifted into all the reasons he's so happy to be marrying her, and all the reasons I'm so happy for him. I love how warm and genuine she is.

Then back to the plans.

"We decided not to have a maid of honor or best man. Her dad will walk her to the chupah, but you and her mom will be the only ones standing under it with us. We just want to honor our moms." *How lucky can one person be?*

"Oh, Jake, I'm touched, but I'd love to have the honor of walking you to the chupah."

"Then you will! This whole thing is to make you happy." How many times and for how many reasons can a person cry in one day?

"Of course we'll do that. You know more about this stuff than I do, would you send us a list of Jewish wedding traditions?" *This is not my imagination, I just heard that, right?*

"You know that book I mentioned, about Jewish weddings? I'll send you a list after I've read it."

"Great. G'night, Mom. Love you."

"Love you too."

I did have a good night. Somehow the wedding joy kept me on an even keel through the evening. Dread dawned with the light of day. Toto? Seemed fine—perky as ever. Chasing deer he never catches, schmoozing with neighbors who always stop to pet him, chowing down on the chicken broth-enhanced dry food I'm offering to keep his weight up. Me? I'm researching probiotics, learning that prednisone's side effects may outweigh its benefits, wondering what it'll be like to watch my pet deteriorate, questioning whether I'll have the stomach and strength to manage his care, and wondering how I'll fare when I come face to face with living alone, without my beloved canine companion. His presence stands between me and the long-dreaded abyss of stark solitude. What will it be like when he's not there, holding up his silent but attentive side of our conversations, empathizing with his deep-set dark chocolate eyes, making me laugh, delighting me by rolling in the grass with abandon, sitting on my lap during thunderstorms, keeping me on track each day—silently standing, staring at me if I forget what time it is, particularly his bedtime snack time.

Just weeks before I was worrying about a loss I'd welcome, when Jake shifts his allegiance and attention to his bride. Jake, the one who bonded with me when his older sisters left for college and has stayed close ever since. Jake, the only one of my children who, after Dan died, was single and free to travel often from L.A. to D.C. On those visits he'd help me around the house, join me on day trips to Monticello, the Blue Ridge

Parkway, outings to local eateries and open-air markets, or just hang out with me at home. Jake, the fun-loving son who's spiced up my life with trips to Maine, Montreal, Big Sur, and more, always coaxing me past my comfort zone, extending his strong hand to me, leading me over jagged steps next to a steep incline, urging "Don't look down, Mom, I've got you."

When I was grappling with grief, overwhelmed by a slew of new tasks, it was Jake who stepped up to help me manage my finances and become my personal 'Car Talk' resource. Jake's engagement—welcome, deeply heartening—heralded a significant change in my life. So, I'd been worrying. *That* was like worrying about how our long-awaited first baby would alter the easy flow of our marriage. Trading one happy state for another.

We had time to prepare, we focused on that—did we have the right outfits, could we borrow a shawl—we checked in with each other, reassured and conferred, and logistics aside, relationship-shifting imminent, counted on gaining strength from our physical closeness, something rare but precious now, taken for granted long ago when we'd shared the same home, blissfully unaware of how brief that time would be in the whole of our lives. Now here we were, the winds having carried us from our separateness to wholeness once more, and we rallied, sharing our strengths, rekindling relationships, remembering rivalries like muscle memory, unwelcome in the rush to support our baby now grown as he stepped into marriage, each of us wondering, pushing back the question, what would the future look like? Realizing this boy had become the last man standing in many of our lives, had slipped into that role as if he'd been rehearsing for it, confidently, caringly, nurturing in his gentle upbeat way, showing up for, bolstering his widowed mom, his suddenly single sister, her fragile preteen daughters, becoming for them what his sisters have been for him but with his own gentle strength and joyful life force.

As he stepped into the life he'd make with his bride, those of us whose lives have been interwoven with his—once the urgency of ceremonial preparations abated—clung to each other for reassurance before breaking away, separating again, remembering and renewing the ways we buffer our separateness, reminded what a distant second it is to sharing one physical space, to embracing, touching, all of our senses filled with each other's presence, energy, familiar uniqueness; reminded what laughing together sounds like—unfiltered by electronics—seeing the eyes twinkle, the laugh lines crinkle, having those unique, viscerally-remembered loved ones close enough to touch, to hug—to savor our connection.

Every cell in me cried out "Yes!" this is where I belong, where I'm known, not only as who I am now but who I came to be; all those years when I was becoming and so were they, knowing me as others never will, loving me unconditionally. Together, celebrating the joy of the youngest in our death-diminished but strong nuclear family—as he shed his singleness to embrace, at last, the woman who'd recognized, as he had, almost instantly, that their long search was over, eager to plunge joyfully into their life together like two kids holding hands, leaping into unknown waters below, confident they'll surface and swim strongly, joyfully, to solid ground.

And the three of us, his older sisters and I, the 'three moms' who remember him before he could crawl, who celebrated his first steps, who hovered nearby till he found his footing; and his nieces—nurtured, sustained, and engaged with him through their teens—return to lives changed by this new phase in his life and ours, feelings raw, emotions swirling, tears surfacing, wondering, hoping, loving, uncertain now of *our* footing, but hopeful, always hopeful, and telling ourselves it will be the same but different; we've done this before, it will be good.

Here Comes Life—I Hope You Like Surprises

Growing up in a classic nineteen-fifties family, I couldn't have imagined occupying a corner office of an organization I'd created, moving across the country to lead a national nonprofit, or losing my husband in the same year I retired. No matter how old I get, life continues to surprise me.

As a child, when our family took a road trip, we expected Dad to drive the whole way. That was true then and continued when my husband and I had a family of our own: I drove carpools and made the local rounds; when we hit the road for a vacation, he took the wheel. That's just the way it was. And it was the man of the house who handled financial decisions and household maintenance. Women's roles were expanding beyond childcare and homemaking, but most women like me had no need to know what was under the hood or inside the fuse box. In high school my girlfriends and I laughed until tears ran down our cheeks when the Driver's Ed teacher expected us to label the parts of the car on the final exam. Why would girls care where the distributor was?

It never occurred to me that I might need to be self-reliant someday. Dad would take care of me till he 'gave me away' at my wedding; then my husband would provide for me, shield me from the business side of life—earning a living, balancing the checkbook, and handling auto or household repairs—somehow magically knowing how to do it himself or how to keep up his end of the conversation with auto mechanics, electricians, and plumbers.

When—surprise—I graduated from college, and—surprise again—had no wedding plans, I found myself in the workforce. Unwilling to accept a secretarial or clerical position, I used my English lit degree to land a job as an editorial assistant at a publishing company. The work came easily—I knew how to catch grammatical and spelling errors—but seeing women in responsible, professional roles? An eye-opener. Collecting a paycheck? Having money of my own? Heady stuff. So what if the corner offices were the exclusive territory of men? It was the sixties; men wore pants, women wore skirts. Placing women in professional roles put my employer ahead of the curve.

A high school girlfriend and I shared an apartment in a trendy area near Chicago's bustling business hub. We were living large, spending what we earned, in a holding pattern until we'd say "I do" and trade business suits for jeans. We spent our paychecks on ourselves and sent our dads the bills for any major expenses. Why save for the future? Prince Charming was just around the corner.

In 1960 *Newsweek* ran a special report investigating the changing lives of educated women. "Who could ask for anything more?" *Newsweek* asked.

> *The educated American woman has her brains, her good looks, her car, her freedom… freedom to choose a dress straight from Paris (original or copy) or attend a class in ceramics or calculus; freedom to determine the timing of her next baby or who shall be the next President of the U.S.*

Although before I married, I'd acquired a taste for engaging with colleagues in a stimulating, often exhilarating workplace, I'd fully expected that 'wife and mother, then grandmother' would define me from the minute I tossed my bouquet till I drew my last breath. From wedding bells to last rites, I thought a man would do the driving—literally and otherwise—while I stayed in conventional women's lanes. Whoa. I can't believe I thought that!

With "Just Married" on our bumper, while pulling away from family and friends in our white Chevy, I remember realizing we were driving into our future. While my husband navigated Chicago's traffic, I wondered, what was ahead?

Twenty years later, guess who occupied the corner office on the twenty-fifth floor of the tallest building in downtown

Houston, loving the job she'd created from whole cloth? In our house I was the one who brought home a paycheck; my spouse was a stay-at-home dad. How about that?

Life continued to unfold in ways I'd never imagined, eventually leading us back to the nation's capital to a dream job for me not listed in O'Net, the Occupational Information Network, creating and leading a U.S. program in a global non-profit, a showcase for an organization largely unknown in the country with the greatest philanthropic resources.

While we never would have guessed that Houston would be our home for twenty-eight years, winding up in the D.C. area with no family nearby would've required an even greater stretch of our imaginations. Then, five years later, months after I'd left that exhilarating but exhausting work to start a consulting practice, another seismic shift: on that bitter cold December morning, my husband walked out the door, called back to me, "I'm going to the store," started the car, and died.

I signed on to the 'till death do us part' pact, but does anyone expect to be the one left standing? Or shift from married to widowed when they feel so vibrant and alive?

At each point in the years that followed I'd take a step forward, then be knocked back—a promising friendship would flounder, an enticing volunteer role would fail to materialize—and I'd be back to square one. But I couldn't give up on forging a new, fulfilling life for myself, so I'd regroup, watch for and push myself to try promising new groups or activities.

Still hoping to pick up the scraps of my career as a consultant, I woke each morning to an empty house and a blank calendar. Whoa. At first it had taken energy and grit to get dressed and face the day. But I pushed myself to hack away at the unwelcome but pressing to-do list that confronts new widows, changing the name on accounts, canceling insurance policies, mailing death certificates—and straining my imagination to arrange some face time each day, even just with store clerks.

Exhausting.

Dispiriting.

But slowly I summoned the energy to do something about my isolation, taking baby steps at first, joining a grief group, then joining other groups where I might find kindred spirits. A hard slog for anyone, much less an emotionally fragile new widow. Slowly, slowly my social calendar filled. One client materialized, followed by another, both short-term projects. Not nearly enough to keep my creative juices flowing. So I had to let go of those last ties to the field that had inspired and defined me.

And, once again the Women's Connection expanded my social circle. Ten years into widowhood I joined a 'peer group' of chapter members in my zip code. That yielded a movie-and-dinner buddy—and the gold ring: a neighbor who's become a close friend and includes me in plans with her wife—doubling the fun and friendship.

The Tree and Me

"They say the tree will die," I told Jake when he visited.

I'd planted that flowering plum tree in Dan's memory soon after he died. I'd always loved this harbinger of Spring. Its pale pink blossoms and bronzed purple leaves would be a striking standout against the green background foliage. Like a bike with training wheels, the fragile seedling was staked to hold it upright until it could stand on its own. But before it found firm footing a mean-spirited storm swept through, leaving it leaning halfway to the ground, hanging on for dear life. I'd just lost my husband of forty-two years. How could Mother Nature take his living memorial?

"The tree expert told me it's hanging on by one root," I told Jake when he visited. "It can't survive."

"Let's give it a chance," he said. He did what he could to straighten it out and secure its moorings. He did the same for me.

"Guess what, Jake?" I called to say, a few years later. "The plum tree's blooming! No wonder it's called an ornamental; it's so beautiful. The trunk is leaning a bit, but it's standing."

The little tree was not just surviving but flourishing. From its slender trunk the branches, covered with wine-colored, sunlight-frosted foliage, form a full, round shape. Scarlet leaves dot the branch-tips with youthful exuberance.

I was blooming too, having weathered the elements of loneliness and idleness and emerged into a new season of my life. Showing up at meetings of civic groups and women's organizations had yielded intellectually engaging projects and, in time, a few close friendships. Summer writing workshops had morphed into the weekly memoir club where 'everybody knows my name' and a whole lot more, as we share raw reflections about our lives. Writing supplies a ticket to ride with creative, supportive, fascinating people. Now when the calendar's empty, I'm glad: more time to write! The practice invites introspection about the sweet and sour ingredients of a life that flew by unexamined.

About that missing ingredient: the plum tree flowered before my friendship with a neighbor germinated; now it's blooming. She emails: "How about a movie Saturday?" Or: "Free for lunch Tuesday?" We sign up, show up or just hang out, especially on weekends.

Today that scrappy sapling towers over the rooftop; its

foliage fills the picture window. Each time Jake visits, he notes with pleasure how 'Daddy's tree' has grown and thrived. So have I.

With the passage of time life flows away from the past and toward what remains to be discovered, enjoyed and woven into a life enriched with unexpected delights and pleasure.

AFTERWORD

Writing Your Next Chapters

When first widowed, struggling to build a new life for myself with the support, but without the proximity of family, I wish I could've known that my many forays into unknown territory would eventually yield a full calendar, close friends, and a regular bridge game with men and women whose friendship extends beyond the card table. And, years after losing my husband, sometimes holidays would find me celebrating in congenial company.

This book chronicles the steps I took, the support I found, and the lessons I learned as, slowly and tentatively at first—starting with my doctor and a psychotherapist—then proactively, joining a grief support group and taking that substantive role on a committee of the Women's Connection—and by showing up at a weekly discussion group, finding a kindred spirit who worked with me to form a book club… the list goes on. The results fill my once-barren social calendar and much more: friends to laugh with, confide in—and, as one of them showed me, share the raw, unprocessed stuff of life.

From the day Dan died I've relied heavily on my adult children, often on matters once in my husband's domain: managing finances, the house, and the car. Each step—from buying a tire to doing my own taxes—was daunting at first but proved to be confidence-building.

None of this was easy. Even now, years later, loneliness still lurks in the shadows, ready to pounce when I spend holidays alone, or when days go by without the company of friends. But I remember when there were no friends nearby—now I have several who know me well and care about me and I care about them. My children keep in constant touch with me; I travel often to see them and my grandchildren, especially to celebrate milestone occasions—theirs and mine. And, to my delight, I'm all in to writing—this book and personal essays—in the company of convivial colleagues. Compared to the barren first years of bereavement, I'm blessed.

Recently I needed emergency surgery. Kay, the friend who'd rescued me the day I became a widow, drove me to the hospital and kept my dog.

Friends emailed: "Do you need groceries?" "Could I stop by with some soup?"

Ah. I'd almost say, "mission accomplished," but I know that someday, in some new situation, I'll be in friend-seeking mode again.

I offer my story to widows finding friends fading away, starting to build a new social circle, learning to navigate life on your own: You're the one embarking on and driving your journey. What will work for you? I can't predict. Push past your comfort zone to find new groups and pursuits. Repeat as needed.

Grief will recede. Letting it go, in your own time, will make room for growth.

Like most journeys, yours will hold surprises, detours, disappointments, and delights. You'll need and you will find co-travelers. Some names and faces will change as you do. Be patient. A new life awaits.

About the Author

After a career as a nonprofit leader expanding opportunities for underserved youth and adults, Barbara turned her passion and pen to creative writing. Her English Literature degree from the University of Michigan served her well, first to advance social change, next to creating narrative nonfiction.

Widowed after forty years of marriage to David, her college sweetheart, Barbara has been navigating widowhood guided by her innate optimism and zest for life. After years of writing workshops, honing her craft in her memoir group, and authoring countless essays, Barbara is delighted to publish her first book, *Oh. I'm a Widow*. A chronicle of her journey, the book offers encouragement, support and guidance to the bereaved.

Mother of three, grandmother of five, Barbara is grateful for her close-knit family and rewarding professional experiences. A native of Chicago and longtime resident of Silver Spring, Maryland, friends and colleagues know her as a woman with a huge heart and hungry intellect. Find Barbara nestled in a Craftsman cottage in the shadow of downtown Los Angeles, living next door to her son and his family. Sample her work at achievingchangetogether.com/published-works

Photograph by Roman Udalov

www.ingramcontent.com/pod-product-compliance
Lightning Source LLC
Chambersburg PA
CBHW052142070526
44585CB00017B/1933